Pre-Season Soccer Training

A Seven Week, 50 Session Guide to Building For The New Season

Vasilis Papadakis

DARK
RIVER

With you, I realize that family is everything for everyone.
So, this book is for you my wife Froso, for you my son Vasilis Junior,
for you my daughter Maria.

Table of Contents

Introduction

The preparation of a soccer team evolves along the lines of one basic principle: "Training is a copy of the real game". Almost all training moments are approached with the use of a ball, in an attempt to simulate match conditions.

From the first day, the ball is at the center of proceedings; its progress across the field influences players' movements, reactions, and thoughts. Improvements in basic and special endurance, coordination, general speed, soccer-specific speed, agility, and even power are undertaken by using a ball. Technical and small-sided games are designed and based on the formation and demands of the tactical approach. In all training sessions, technical, tactical, physical and psychological components (e.g., the four corner approach) are included, as essential constituents.

In terms of structure and content, the first week is "introductory" and seeks to incorporate players into the team's philosophy and coaching approach. The content gives players the opportunity to "get acquainted" with the program and develop a willingness to work and exert effort. It has been designed, based on the premise that footballers have followed an off-season training program over the summer. The second and third weeks focus on improving basic strength-endurance. In turn, the first three weeks have a basic requirement to improve strength with core power exercises and multi-arc exercises, with and without the ball. The fourth and fifth weeks focus on special soccer endurance. From the fifth week onwards, we train more specifically with regard to speed and speedpower (soccer power).

The sixth and seventh weeks take the form of a microcycle in a championship season, preparing and "shaping" the players for their championship matches. In all the training sessions, previous objectives are approached in relation to the tactics and the formation of the team. Consistent approaches to thinking, teaching, training, and implementation are provided every day.

A key element in the process – as something that will improve, evolve, and give strength and impetus – is the importance given to the meaning of the words "TEAM" and "FAMILY". Players learn the power that everyone can give or add to the team, and this power enables team members to become better and more efficient. "TEAM-FAMILY" is an essential objective with respect to relationships, the acceptance of idiosyncrasies, and a willingness to adapt to rules. Not as some kind of enforcement, but as a conscious need!

Special Comments

Based on players' goals and capabilities, my aim as a coach when I developed the program was to create a team that attempts to play fast aggressive football, which dominates on the pitch, and which presses the opposition a lot. For this reason, two formations were chosen and developed – a 1-4-2-3-1 and a 1-4-3-3; a 1-4-4-2 diamond was also utilized sporadically.

These formations combined mobility and created width. They were used to create space, and enable the participation of a good number of players in the final phase thanks to the exploitation of full-backs as an extra player in the play's build-up. The use of set pieces, and the creation of shots, are elements that will be emphasized, due to the characteristics of the team's players. In defense, my focus was on direct and constant pressure on the ball holder, the diagonal cover of teammates, the short distance between the players and the lines, and player communication; indeed, these are the basic elements that we will work on. A lot of attention will be given to defensive marking in the static phases and proper placement in the penalty area when we make crosses from the side. Defensively and offensively, the team will try to exploit players' capabilities in 1vs1 scenarios, and we will aggressively try to bring the three players behind the No 9 into the penalty area through combined mobility, and back and diagonal passes.

The sessions are daily, some are duplicated (weeks two to five), there is a friendly match every Saturday, and each Sunday offers a day off for rest.

The Full Programme

WEEK	MONDAY	TUESDAY	WEDNESDAY	THURSDAY	FRIDAY	SATURDAY	SUNDAY
week 1	BASIC SOCCER ENDURANCE TACTICS CORE POWER	BASIC SOCCER ENDURANCE TACTICS CORE POWER	BASIC SOCCER ENDURANCE TACTICS CORE POWER	BASIC SOCCER ENDURANCE TACTICS CORE POWER	BASIC SOCCER ENDURANCE TACTICS CORE POWER	FRIENDLY MATCH	REST
week 2	BASIC SOCCER POWER BASIC SOCCER ENDURANCE TACTICS	BASIC SOCCER ENDURANCE TACTICS	BASIC SOCCER POWER BASIC SOCCER ENDURANCE TACTICS	BASIC SOCCER ENDURANCE TACTICS	BASIC SOCCER POWER BASIC SOCCER ENDURANCE TACTICS	FRIENDLY MATCH	REST
week 3	BASIC SOCCER ENDURANCE TACTICS	BASIC SOCCER POWER BASIC SOCCER ENDURANCE TACTICS	BASIC SOCCER ENDURANCE TACTICS	BASIC SOCCER POWER BASIC SOCCER ENDURANCE TACTICS	BASIC SOCCER ENDURANCE TACTICS	FRIENDLY MATCH	REST
week 4	SOCCER POWER BASIC SOCCER ENDURANCE TACTICS	SPECIAL SOCCER ENDURANCE TACTICS	SOCCER POWER BASIC SOCCER ENDURANCE TACTICS	SPECIAL SOCCER ENDURANCE TACTICS	SOCCER POWER SPEED BASIC SOCCER ENDURANCE TACTICS	FRIENDLY MATCH	REST
week 5	BASIC SOCCER ENDURANCE TACTICS	SPEED SOCCER SPEED BASIC SOCCER ENDURANCE TACTICS	SPECIAL SOCCER ENDURANCE TACTICS	SOCCER SPEED BASIC SOCCER ENDURANCE TACTICS	SPECIAL SOCCER ENDURANCE TACTICS	FRIENDLY MATCH	REST
week 6	SPECIAL SOCCER ENDURANCE TACTICS	SPEED TACTICS	TACTICS	SOCCER POWER TACTICS	TACTICS	FRIENDLY MATCH	REST
week 7	BASIC SOCCER ENDURANCE TACTICS	REST	SOCCER-SPEED SPECIAL SOCCER ENDURANCE TACTICS	TACTICS	REACTION SPEED TACTICS	REST	League Game

Diagram Key

Player moves with the ball:

Player moves without the ball:

The ball is passed/moves:

Week 1

MONDAY	TUESDAY	WEDNESDAY	THURSDAY	FRIDAY	SATURDAY	SUNDAY
BASIC SOCCER ENDURANCE	BASIC SOCCER ENDURANCE	BASIC SOCCER ENDURANCE	BASIC SOCCER ENDURANCE	BASIC SOCCER ENDURANCE	FRIENDLY MATCH	REST
TACTICS	TACTICS	TACTICS	TACTICS	TACTICS		
CORE POWER	CORE POWER	CORE POWER	CORE POWER	CORE POWER		

The first week is all about preparing the players – in conjunction with benchmark tests (power, fitness, and strength) and player-specific planning – for the next few weeks. The workouts are aerobic, through passing games and technical exercises. Core power exercises are incorporated, and the first tactical instructions are given. Namely, we focus on:

- Player mobility
- Establishing diagonal relationships, with depth, between players
- 'Transition as thought' (when the ball is won or lost, players should think immediately about what they need to do next)
- Defensive depth and aggressive width
- Changes of direction during gameplay

In passing games, in this first week, we are *not* looking for intense effort, and we restrict physical contact to avoid excessive physical strain and duelling between players (we don't want players picking up injuries in week one!). At the end of the week, we have our first friendly game, which all our players will take part in; no player, preferably, shall have more than 45 minutes of game time.

Session 1 | Monday

Warm up

We start with a passing drill on a 50m x 30m pitch. Use subgroups of 7-8 players, with one ball for every team. Players are assigned specific numbers, starting from 1 to 7 (or 8, if you have 8 players).

All players shall run slowly in the space, passing the ball in the specified order: 1 to 2, 2 to 3, etc. They should vary how they pass and include right foot, left foot, alternate feet, one or two touches - all depending on the coach's instructions. Play for 2 x 7-minute periods, with a 2-minute break in-between.

Main part

Begin with 8-10 minutes of exercises, incorporating dynamic stretching. Then put on a small-sided passing game in three teams of 7-8 players. The pitch is 40 x 30 m.

The third team (yellow in the illustration above) shall act as additional players to whichever team is in possession of the ball. The players on the pitch play with 2 or 3 touches, maximum. Outside players are only allowed one or two touches (wall pass, or receive and pass). Play should take place for 3 x 7 minute periods, with a 2-minute break in-between games.

Limiting time on the ball and contact with the ball is the aim of the game; in addition, players are forced to assess what they see in front of them quickly, and they need to make decisions quickly.

Coaching

Emphasise:

1. Continuous movement, in the space, by non-ball holders to provide passing options for the player in possession
2. The diagonal relationships of the players
3. Pressure on the ball holder
4. Short distances between members of the defending team (e.g., ensure they stay compact), whilst there should be a "spread" (e.g., width) by the attacking team
5. There is a focus on moments of transition, mainly to develop fast reactions and repositioning by players

Follow Up Session

Core Stability Exercises. 2 x 8 minutes. Exercise time of 20 seconds with a break of 2 minutes between sets.

1. Front plank
2. Side left plank
3. Rear plank
4. Side right plank
5. Abdominals
6. Superman Exercises (for back muscles)
7. Push-ups
8. Russian Twists

Recovery

6 minutes of slow running on the field, and 5-6 minutes of passive stretching

Warm up

A passing drill in a 20 x 20m box, using subgroups of 5-8 players. Time 2 x 7 minutes, with a change of direction for the second half. Break for 2 minutes in-between.

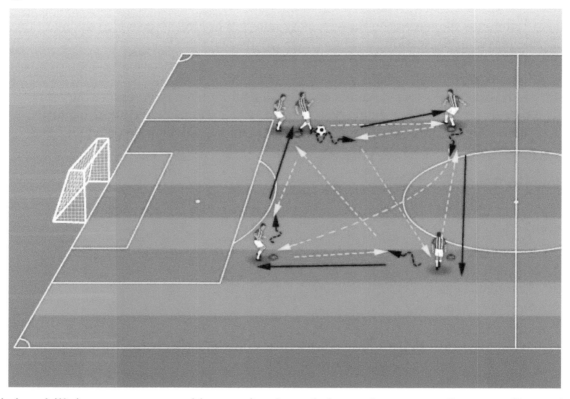

This is a drill that generates aerobic exercise through forward passes, wall passes, diagonal passes, and the players changing position following their passes.

Main part

- 8-10 minutes of dynamic exercises
- A small-sided passing game, with 6 (or a maximum of 8) cones representing the 'target'(s) for each group. Use subgroups of 8 (up to 10) players on a pitch of 40 x 50m. Time 2 x 7 minutes with a 3-minute break at halftime

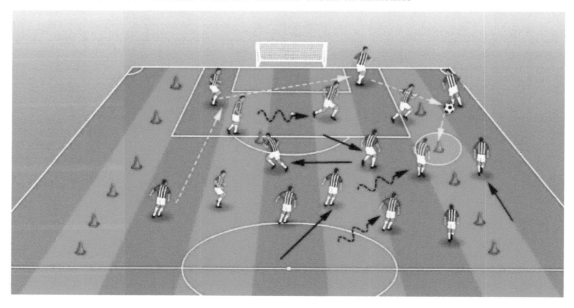

This is a passing game with each team defending or going after 6 (max 8) cones. The goal is to hit the ball into an opposition cone through combination play. When a player hits the ball into an opponent's cone, he must pick up the cone and take it over to his side. While holding and carrying the cone, he cannot take part in the game and thus a small-overload is created for a few seconds. The space behind the cones plays normally, as shown in the figure. The winning team has the most cones!

Coaching

Emphasise

1. Continuous movement in free space to provide options for the ball holder
2. The diagonal relationships between the players
3. Pressure on the ball holder
4. Short distances between members of the defending team, and width for the attackers
5. *Really* emphasize the importance of transitions, in order to develop fast reactions and player movements

Follow Up Session

A 2 x 7 minute running drill comprising of 30 seconds of hard running followed by 30 seconds of slower running (For example, 30 seconds of hard running to cover 140m, then 30 seconds of slower running to cover 70m – the aim being to develop players' vVO2max) with a 3 minute break in the middle.

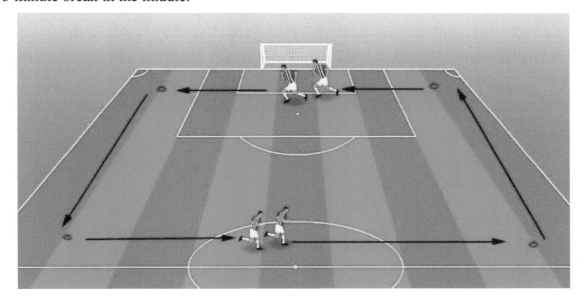

Follow Up Session II

10 minutes of core stability exercises. Exercise time of 20 seconds per station.

1. Front plank
2. Side left plank
3. Rear plank
4. Side right plank
5. Abdominals
6. Superman Exercises (for back muscles)
7. Push-ups
8. Russian Twists

Recovery

6 minutes of slow running around the field, then 5-6 minutes of passive stretching.

Session 3 | Wednesday

Warm up

2 x 7 minutes of a formation-based passing drill (highlighting positional technique). Every player follows his pass, so they change position after every pass. The player at the end of the move must dribble the ball to the start. Variation: two touches, one touch.

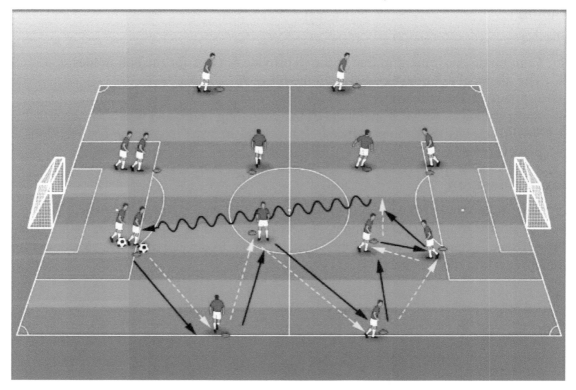

Coaching

- Correct body position
- Angle to the ball
- Receiving the ball correctly and pass quality
- Reverse movements

Main part

1. 8-10 minutes of dynamic stretching in 2 subgroups
2. Small-sided passing game, from an external target player to an external target player. There needs to be a minimum of 6 passes for a goal to count. If the ball is lost, the winning team transfers it to an external player, to start the count again. Time 3 x 8 minutes, with a 2-minute break between games

Coaching

- Attacking width and depth
- Changes of side (e.g., a big pass from the left central defender to the right full back; or a long pass from a defensive midfielder to a wide attacker on the other side of field)
- Defensive organization with pressure on the ball holder and teammate cover
- Fast reactions to any change in phase/transition (e.g., from possession to losing the ball)

Follow Up Session

10 minutes of core stability work. Each station is 25 seconds.

1. Front plank
2. Side left plank
3. Rear plank
4. Side right plank
5. Abdominals
6. Superman Exercises (for back muscles)
7. Push-ups
8. Russian Twists

Follow Up Session II

An 8-minute running drill comprised of 60 seconds of hard running followed by 60 seconds of less hard running. The distances to be run will depend on the fitness levels of the players (as determined by the benchmark tests from earlier in the week). For example, if we have two subgroups, Group 1 might have to run 220m in 60 seconds, followed by 110m in 60 seconds, for 8 minutes. Group 2, on the other hand, runs for 230m in 60 seconds, and 115m in 60 seconds for 8 minutes.

Recovery

6 minutes of slow running on the field, then 5-6 minutes of passive stretching.

Session 4 | Thursday

Warm up

8 minutes of passing in pairs, using free moves in space, and over distances of 5-6m between players. Variations: Right foot, left foot, one touch, two touches, overlap.

After the passing drill is complete, carry out 10 minutes of dynamic stretching exercises.

Main part

A small-sided passing game in a 60 x 40m playing space divided into 2 zones, with 3 teams of 7-8 players. It's a game of aggressive overloads and defensive underloads 7 vs 5 (8 vs 6). The defenders try to steal the ball and take it to the opposite zone. Whilst two players from the defending team stay where they are (they should be different players each time), the remaining players in the team will follow into the opposite zone. The third team practices core power exercises. Time 3 x 7 minutes, change roles every 7 minutes and break for 2 minutes in-between.

Coaching

Attack:

- The creation of attacking width and depth
- Teammate support
- Small and longer pass variations
- Possession

Defence:

- Pressure on the ball holder
- Diagonal defensive teammate cover
- Anticipating passes, and closing down short passes
- Communication

Note: Defensive and attacking transitions should be each player's main thoughts!

Follow Up Session

30 seconds of high-speed running followed by 30 seconds of slow running (in subgroups) for 8 minutes.

Follow Up Session II

10 minutes of core stability exercises.

Follow Up Session III

(The same as Follow Up Session I) - 30 seconds of high-speed running followed by 30 seconds of slow running (in subgroups) for 8 minutes.

Recovery

6 minutes of slow running around the field, followed by 5-6 minutes of passive stretching.

Warm up

A passing drill 2 x 7 minutes with a 3-minute break in-between. Subgroups of 8 players. Field 30 x 20 m.

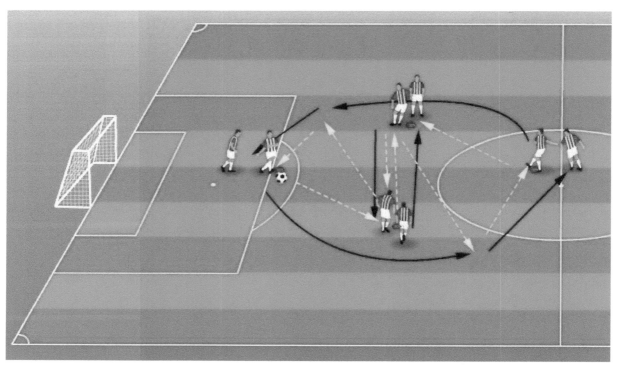

This is an overlap-moves drill, with two players at every station; change player positions at each station during the break.

Main part

- 10 minutes of dynamic stretching
- A small-sided passing game on a 50 x 40m pitch, comprised of three teams of 7-8 players. The third team will be running drills or core stability exercises. Time 3 x 7 minutes with a 2-minute break in-between

Coaching

1. Continuous movement and repositioning, in relation to whomever is in possession of the ball
2. When the ball holder's team is in possession, all his/her teammates should make themselves available for a pass. The full size of the playing space should be used, and players should not all stand too close to the ball
3. When defending:

    a. Pressure on the ball holder

    b. Cover (diagonal-triangles)

    c. Communication (Me! Go! You!)

4. Consistency is important here; there should be small distances between the players and the lines!

Main part II

A game for 10 minutes on a field of 90 x 60 m. With goalkeepers.

Coaching

1. When in your defensive half, a player has a maximum of two touches
2. Players need to be secure when on the ball, and avoid risk
3. When defending, support should be in depth
4. The goalkeepers should be used as extra outfield players, as appropriate!
5. The ball should be switched from side to side to find space
6. The defensive line should press
7. Encourage free play and creativity when attacking

Follow Up Session

An 8-minute running drill, 52 seconds of slow running followed by an 8-second sprint.

Recovery

6 minutes of slow running around the field and 5-6 minutes of passive stretching.

Session 6 | Saturday

Warm up

Match warm up; 25-30 minutes as follows:

- 4 minutes of free movement in pairs with passes
- 6 minutes of dynamic stretching
- 2 x 3-minute passing game; 5 vs 5
- 4 minutes of crossing and shooting in formation pairs
- 3 minutes of shots around the penalty area (three per player)
- Reaction sprints; 6 repetitions over 8 metres

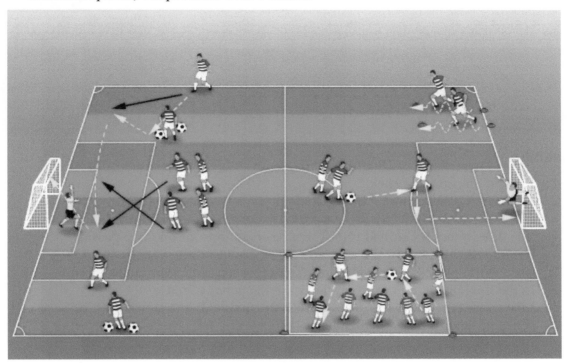

Main part

A friendly match for 90 minutes. Each player should get at least 45 minutes of game time. Different formations should be used in each half.

First half: Formation 1-4-2-3-1

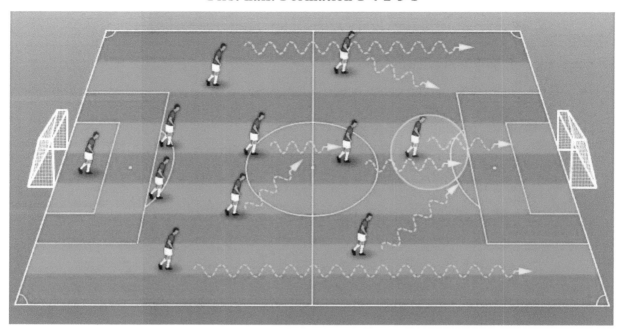

Coaching

1. Playing out from the back
2. Utilization of full-backs when attacking
3. One defensive midfielder always provides cover (stays behind the ball)
4. The three attackers around "No 9" create conditions for one-two passing
5. Central players support the attackers for overloads, through balls, or shots
6. The central players provide "hidden" movements around the attackers (rotation)
7. In the final phase, aim for four players in the penalty area
8. Line consistency (e.g., the lines of defence, midfield, and attack must be clear and cohesive when a team is defending)

Second half: Formation 1-4-4-2 (Diamond)

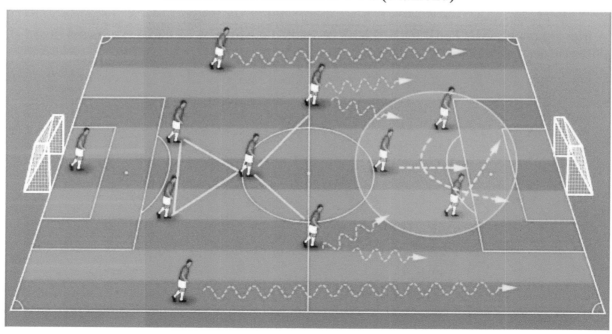

Coaching

1. Play out from the back, and use the full-backs when attacking
2. The defensive midfielder always takes care of the two most important defensive triangles (1: With two central defenders, he is at the top of triangle; with two central midfielders, he is at the bottom of triangle)
3. Opposing moves of two strikers
4. The player at the top of the diamond moves as a "hidden" attacker
5. The three attackers work together to assist shots on goal or vertical passes
6. Line consistency (e.g., the lines of defence, midfield, and attack must be clear and cohesive when a team is defending)

Defensive directions (common)

Pressure the ball holder, offer diagonal cover and defensive depth. Anticipate passes. Provide a short passing option.

Recovery

6 minutes of slow running around the field and 5-6 minutes of passive stretching   .

Day 7 | Sunday | Rest

Week 2

MONDAY	TUESDAY	WEDNESDAY	THURSDAY	FRIDAY	SATURDAY	SUNDAY
BASIC SOCCER POWER	BASIC SOCCER ENDURANCE	BASIC SOCCER POWER	BASIC SOCCER ENDURANCE	BASIC SOCCER POWER	FRIENDLY MATCH	REST
BASIC SOCCER ENDURANCE	TACTICS	BASIC SOCCER ENDURANCE	TACTICS	BASIC SOCCER ENDURANCE		
TACTICS		TACTICS		TACTICS		

For the second week, we start to utilise double sessions (morning and afternoon), with the three morning sessions aiming to improve player power. In the afternoon, we shall look to improve aerobic fitness through technical exercises and small-sided games. Technique and agility are also covered. With regard to tactical themes, we focus on ball-oriented "spatial" defence and defence-to-attack transitions. We aggressively seek and direct the build-up of play from defence, involving full backs, and we start to develop the roles and positioning of players in the final phase of play. At the end of the week, the second friendly match takes place, involving all the players.

Session 7 | Monday (Morning)

Warm up

10 minutes of dynamic stretching. 4 minutes of passing, in pairs, at high pace.

Main part

Power exercises comprising of 25 seconds at 10 stations. 2 sets. Total time 40 minutes.

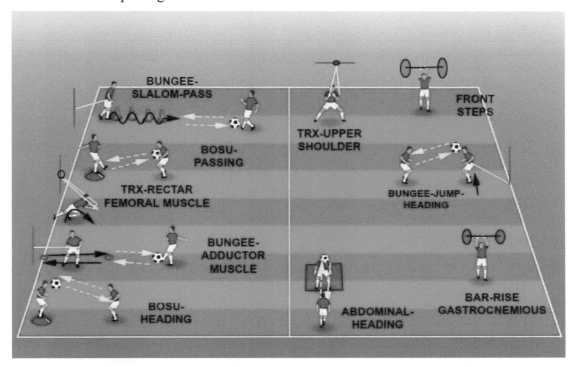

1. Bungee slalom moves and passing
2. Bosu skipping and passing with foot changes
3. TRX exercise for femoral muscle development
4. Bungee side-steps and passing
5. Bosu skipping and heading
6. Abdominals heading
7. Foot-rises with a bar
8. Bungee-jump-heading
9. Bar front steps
10. TRX upper zone

After each exercise, each player has to run, at speed, for 15m.

Recovery

8 minutes of slow running followed by 6 minutes of passive stretching.

Session 8 | Monday (Afternoon)

Warm up

A 10 minute Rondo, 5 vs 2.

One player presses, one covers.

10 minutes of agile movements and stretching in two subgroups

Main part

A passing game 10 vs 8 (+2) with the emphasis on transition. Use half of the field in two zones. When the ball is dispossessed, change positions and roles. Each time, two players must stay in the other zone to create overloads and underloads. Time 2 x 8 minutes.

Main part II

A small-sided game in a three-zone field. Space 70 x 60m. (three zones of 25 x 60 m). Attacking zone 3 vs 3, defensive zone, 3 vs 3, middle zone 4 vs 4. Time 2 x 8 minutes, with a break of 4 minutes in-between.

Coaching

Defence:

1. Pressure on the ball holder
2. Diagonal cover
3. Communication: (Me! You! Go! Close!)

Attack:

1. Stay wide to take advantage of free space
2. Emphasis on one-two passing (support and movement)

Follow Up Session

An 8-minute running drill, 52 seconds of slow running followed by an 8-second sprint.

Recovery

4 minutes of slow running then 6 minutes of passive stretches.

Warm up

A 20-minute exercise of dynamic stretching (8-9 minutes) and drills that focus on passing, receiving the ball, and slalom moves (for 10 minutes).

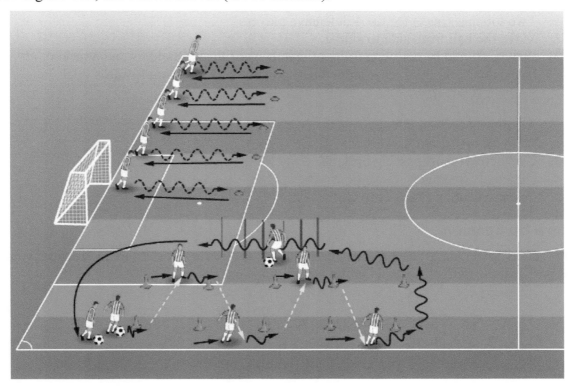

Main part

A 10 v s10 possession game, time 3 x 8 minutes, in a space of 70 x 60m. For the first two sessions, you should have a passing game with a passive defence (players close the space but do not make active tackles); afterwards, the defence should be active. Rotate the teams every 8 minutes.

Coaching

1. Build-up using small and medium-length passes
2. Encourage diagonal relationships between players
3. Maintain line consistency (defence, midfield, attack)

Attack:

1. Two touches (max) for the 4 defensive players
2. Move the ball from side to side
3. Players should be active in order to create space for midfielders and attackers
4. In the attacking third, encourage one-two passes or dribbling towards goal

Defence (passive):

1. A compact line of defence
2. Pressure on the ball holder
3. Close down short passing options
4. Diagonal coverage
5. Communication (Me! You! Go! Close!)

Follow Up Session

A 15-minute attacking drill with four player subgroups (vertical passes to central attackers, wall passes backwards, diagonal middle passes, crossing, shots on goal).

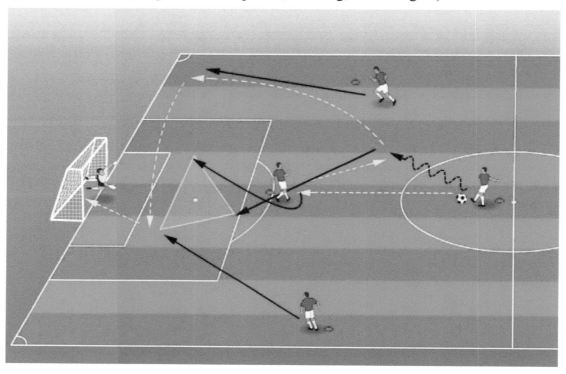

Coaching

1. Vertical passes to an attacker
2. Quality wall passes, so the midfielder can play the game with one touch
3. Movement away from the attacker – from a teammate – in order to create space
4. Diagonal passes in space, in front of a teammate so he can 'accelerate' onto the ball
5. A triangular arrangement of attackers in the keeper's area (e.g. one in front of the goalie, one to the side, and one behind the first player)
6. Controlled movements, so that there is sudden movement (e.g., sprint), after the final pass

Follow Up Session II

An 8-minute running drill; 30 seconds of sprinting followed by 30 seconds of slower running, in subgroups.

Recovery

2 minutes of slow running followed by 6 minutes of stretching.

Session 10 | Wednesday (Morning)

Warm up

12 minutes of dynamic stretching exercises.

Main part

Power exercises comprising of 25 seconds at 10 stations. Two sets. Total time 40 minutes.

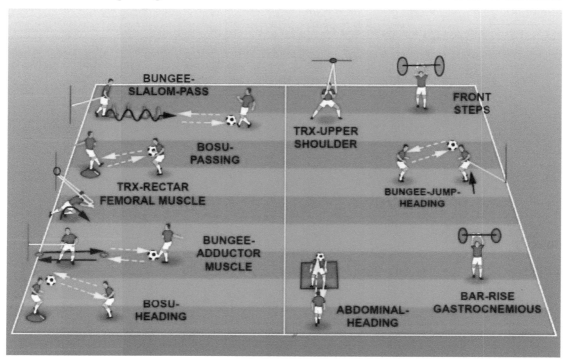

1. Bungee slalom moves and passing
2. Bosu skipping and passing with foot changes
3. TRX exercise for femoral muscle
4. Bungee side-steps and passing
5. Bosu skipping and heading
6. Abdominals heading
7. Foot-rises with a bar
8. Bungee-jump-heading
9. Bar front steps
10. TRX upper zone

After each exercise, each player has to run, at speed, for 15m.

Note: Between the two sets, have a 4-minute energy break. Get the players in a small circle and play the ball in the air, with free touches in 3-4 subgroups.

Recovery

8 minutes of slow running then 4 minutes of passive stretching.

Session 11 | Wednesday (Afternoon)

Warm up

6 minutes of active stretching, in pairs.

12 minutes of coordination work with the ball (3 stations, time 3 minutes x 3. Break for 1 minute).

Station 1 - wall passes

Station 2 - heading

Station 3 - double passes in the air

Main part

Game 8 vs 8 (with 2 neutral players). Time 8 minutes. Pitch size of 60 x 40m.

Coaching

Players have 2-3 touches, whilst the neutrals have a maximum of 2.

Attack:

- Open up the spaces on the field
- Diagonal support relationships, utilising width and depth
- Quality passing
- Combined mobility

Defence:

- Pressure on the ball holder
- Close down short passing options
- Diagonal coverage
- Stay compact. Deny space to the attackers
- Communication: (Me! You! Go! Close!)

Follow Up Session

A slightly different game of 8 vs 8 + 2 external players (target players) on a field of 60 x 40m. External target players change every 2 minutes.

Coaching

The aim of the game is to transfer the ball from one side of the pitch to the other, with a minimum of 6 passes (not counting the outside players). We always start with an outside player. When one team dispossesses the other, we have to pass to an outside player to start the next set.

- Diagonal support relationships (triangles)
- A focus on vertical football: reaching the goal

Defence:

- Pressure on the ball holder
- Close down nearby passing choices

- Good communication with each other

Follow Up Session II

2 x 8 minutes of running: 30 seconds fast, 30 seconds slow, in three subgroups.

Recovery

Two circuits of slow running then 6 minutes of stretching.

Session 12 | Thursday

Warm up

10-minute passing drill – give and go – to improve 1-4-2-3-1 positioning.

Emphasis on:

- The correct body angle, relative to the ball
- The quality of the pass
- Reverse movements

To run the drill, use 2-4 balls at a time.

Follow up the passing drill with 10 minutes of mobility-agility.

Main part

A small-sided game with four small goals. Pitch of 50 x 30m for 2 x 8 minutes. Break for 3 minutes.

In this passing game, each team defends two small goals.

Coaching

Emphasis is placed on:

- Continuous movement in the space to provide options and support to the ball holder
- The diagonal relationships of the players
- The compactness of the defending team
- The width of the attacking team
- Mobility when in possession

We emphasize transition as thought (when the ball is won or lost, players should think immediately about what they need to do next, tactically).

Follow Up Session

A 10 vs 10 game in zones. Space 80 x 50m with defence and attack zones of 25 x 50m, and a middle zone that is 30 x 50m. In the middle zone, you have a 4 vs 3 situation; in the others, a 4 vs 2 defensive overload. Time 2 x 8 minutes. The two teams compete with different formations: 1-4-4-2 and 1-4-3-3. We have two different scenarios in defence and – based on these – we try:

1. With three attackers (1 central attacker); take advantage of the free centre back to create 2 vs 1 situations
2. With two attackers (2 central attackers); utilise one midfielder to create a 3 vs 2 situation. In both cases, the full backs are high up the pitch

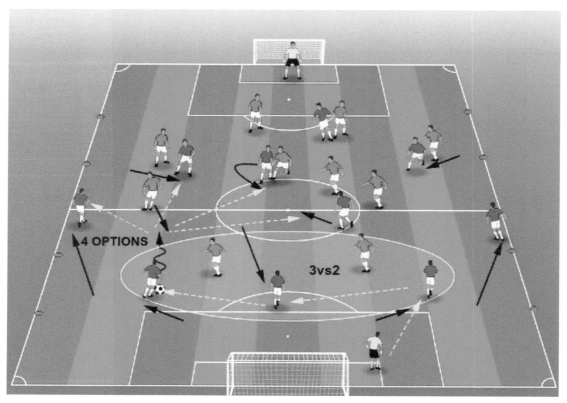

When the opposing team plays with two attackers, utilise one defensive midfielder, and create 3 vs 2 situations.

When the opposing team uses one attacker, then we put him in the middle, to create a 2 vs 1 to start our build-up.

Coaching

With the main goal of developing play from the back, we focus on:

- Deploying the four defenders with depth, with two central defenders for safe passing
- Ensuring that passes are completed
- Using our goalkeeper to help move the ball
- Creating deliberately weakened sides
- Pushing forward from the back, into the next zone, to create a 5 vs 4 overload
- Defensive high pressure to disrupt the passing of the ball (due to overloads)

Follow Up Session II

An 8-minute running drill 1 vs 1; time 20 seconds fast, 40 second break, in three subgroups.

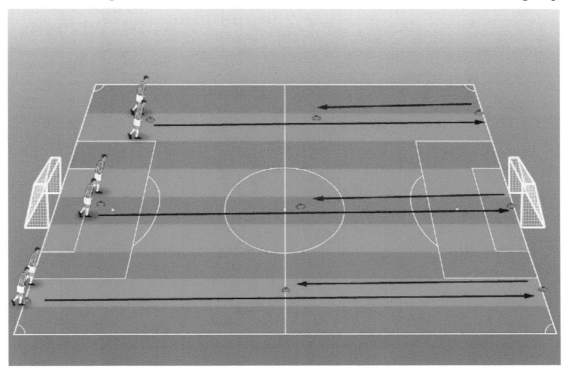

Recovery

8 minutes of slow running followed by 6 minutes of passive stretching.

Session 13 | Friday (Morning)

Warm up

8 minutes of dynamic stretching followed by 4 minutes of passing in pairs at high pace.

Main part

Power exercises. 25 seconds at 10 stations, Two sets. Total time 40 minutes.

Have a break between sets of 4 minutes when players keep the ball in the air with unlimited contacts in 2-3 subgroups.

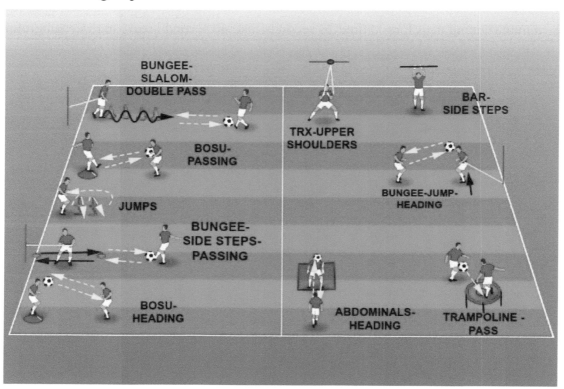

1. Bungee slalom moves and passing
2. Bosu skipping and passing with foot changes
3. Continuous jumps
4. Bungee side-steps and passing
5. Bosu skipping and heading
6. Abdominals heading
7. Trampoline passing
8. Bungee-jump-heading
9. Bar front steps
10. TRX upper zone

Follow Up Session

Pro-Speed drills. Time 8 minutes.

In this exercise, you are preparing the players for speed training. 8 stations of 20m each:

1. Rhythmic jumps alternate
2. Skating (ladder steps)
3. Sneaks (heels up whilst running)
4. Change of direction at speed
5. Reverse steps (backwards)
6. Two rotational turns
7. Diagonal jumps on one leg
8. Sprint for 20m.

Aim for proper execution at each station.

Recovery

8 minutes of slow running around the field followed by 5 minutes of passive stretching.

Session 14 | Friday (Afternoon)

Warm up

6 minutes of active stretching followed by 12 minutes of co-ordinated footwork across 5 stations. Time 3 x 6 minutes, with a 1-minute break in-between.

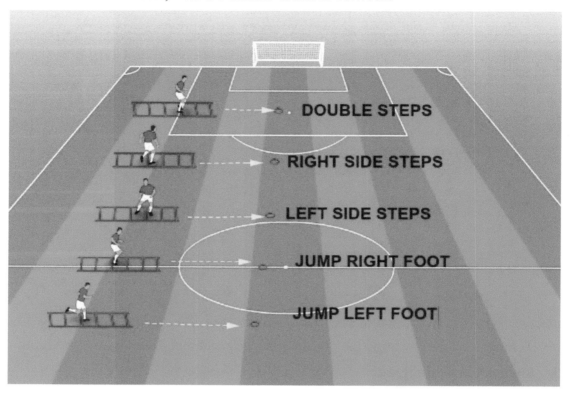

Main part

A small-sided game on a 60 x 40m field, with four external zones and one target player in every zone. Time 3 x 8 minutes.

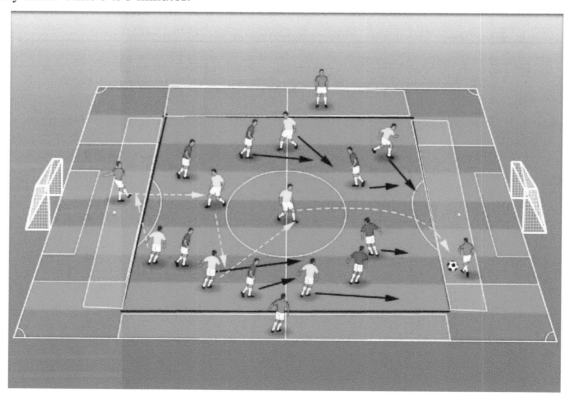

Coaching

This is a special passing game, aimed at changing play in the space, and adapting to new conditions (transitions to attack and defence). Start as a normal possession game where the player in possession receives the ball in a neutral space where he won't be pressed. With two touches, he now has to change the side of play with a big pass to 1 of 4 outside players.

The outside players have to:

- Quickly understand what is happening in front of them
- Receive the ball well
- Make quality passes/transfers to inside players

In-field players have three touches; outside players have two touches. Change the outside players every 8 minutes or when there is a natural break in the game.

Follow Up Session

An 8-minute running drill; 7 seconds of hard sprinting followed by 53 seconds of slower running, in 3 subgroups.

Follow Up Session II

6 minutes of 20 second fast, 20-second slow running, in 3 subgroups.

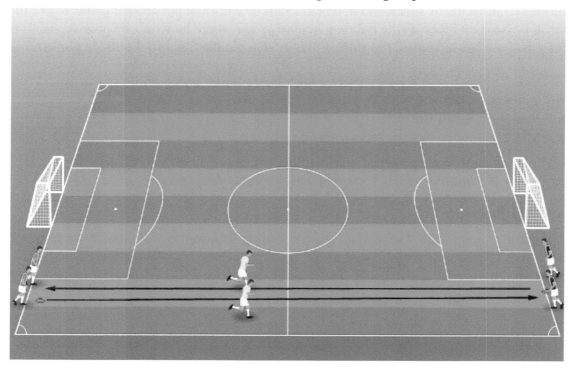

Each subgroup starts when the other arrives.

Recovery

8 minutes of passive stretching.

Session 15 | Saturday

Match time. 45 minutes for each player.

Attempt to apply general basic tactical features:

Defensive function:

- Line Consistency
- Pressure on the ball holder – Teammates should provide diagonal cover, and everyone should communicate
- Defensive transition
- 'Full on' pressing for 5-6 seconds once the opposition wins the ball

Attacking focus:

- Line Consistency
- Continuous motion. Supporting players should offer continuous movement around the No 9!
- Full-backs. Play up the pitch.
- Penalty area: three players in!

Formations 1-4-2-3-1 and 1-4-3-3

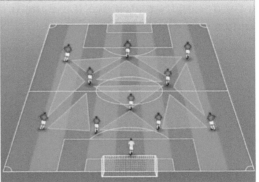

Day 14 | Sunday | Rest

Week 3

MONDAY	TUESDAY	WEDNESDAY	THURSDAY	FRIDAY	SATURDAY	SUNDAY
BASIC SOCCER ENDURANCE	BASIC SOCCER POWER	BASIC SOCCER ENDURANCE	BASIC SOCCER POWER	BASIC SOCCER ENDURANCE	FRIENDLY MATCH	REST
TACTICS	BASIC SOCCER ENDURANCE	TACTICS	BASIC SOCCER ENDURANCE	TACTICS		
	TACTICS		TACTICS			

In the third week, we'll perform two more morning training sessions, with strength and speed content. With afternoon training, we will look to improve aerobic fitness – mainly through possession games – whilst special endurance is also introduced. Training focuses on ball-oriented defence, through drills and small-sided games.

We shall also develop putting pressure on the ball holder, switching phases (transition), and the compactness of player lines. We'll put together aggressive tactics and place an emphasis on where players position themselves and how they should finish the attacking phase (scoring opportunities, through different moves and interchanges). At the end of the week, we add aggressive set pieces for attack.

In our third friendly match, we'll use the first XI players for 60 minutes and the second XI for 30 minutes.

Warm up

8 minutes of active stretching in pairs, and free passing moves in the penalty area.

12 minutes of a small-medium passing drill, in subgroups of 7 players. Area 30 x 15m. Time 2 x 6 minutes. Rotate whoever is in the middle.

Try for a one-touch passing game! The emphasis is on passing quality. You can chop things up depending on the number of players you have.

Main part

A passing game, 10vs10, time 3 x 8 minutes, on a 70 x 60 m pitch. For the first two passing games, utilize a passive defence but remember to change roles for the second session. For the third session, the defence should become active.

Coaching

1. Build-up play with small and medium passes
2. Ensure good diagonal relationships between players
3. Enforce line consistency

Attacking

- Two contacts (max) from the four defenders as the buildup starts
- Encourage players to change sides
- Get mobile! Midfielders and attackers need to create space
- One-two passes and penetration into the final third of the pitch

Defence (passive):

- Line and player compactness
- Pressure on the ball holder
- Offer close range / short passing options
- Diagonal coverage
- Great communication

Follow Up Session

A 10 minute drill to develop overlapping moves in subgroups of three players. An emphasis on the final pass and shoot.

Subgroups of three players and overlap moves using half the pitch. The final pass should come from the player who starts in the middle. Change roles every set.

Follow Up Session II

An 8 minute running drill – 30 seconds fast, 30 seconds slow – in subgroups.

Recovery

Two sets of slow running, on the field, followed by 6 minutes of passive stretching.

Session 17 | Tuesday (morning)

Warm up

6 minutes of energetic stretching, then 8 minutes of technique practice in subgroups of three players.

Main part

Power exercises comprising of 30 seconds at 10 stations. Total time 30 minutes.

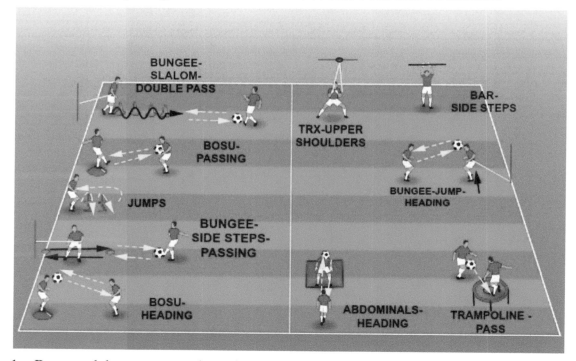

1. Bungee slalom moves and passing
2. Bosu skipping and passing with foot changes

3. Continuous jumping
4. Bungee side-steps and passing
5. Bosu skipping and heading
6. Abdominals heading
7. Trampoline passing
8. Bungee-jump-heading
9. Bar side steps
10. TRX – upper zone

After each exercise, the player does a 20 metre speed run, with a change of direction.

Follow Up Session

Pro-speed drill (preparing for speed training) by Chr. Mourikis. Time 10 minutes.

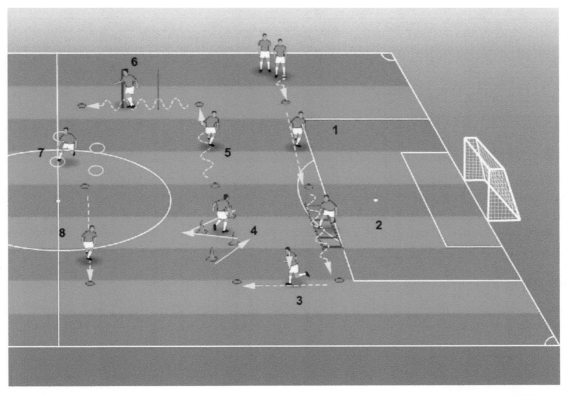

In this exercise, you are preparing the players for speed training at eight stations of 20 metres each:

1. Rhythmic jumps alternate
2. Skating (ladder steps)
3. Sneaks
4. Change direction speed
5. Reverse steps (backwards)
6. Two Rotational turns
7. Diagonal jumps on one leg
8. Sprint 20 m.

Aim for proper execution at each station!

Recovery

8 minutes of slow running then 6 minutes of stretching.

Warm up

6 minutes of active stretching and mobility, followed by a 14 minute passing drill (ball-space defence) in 1vs1 and 2vs2 situations.

The aim of this exercise is to develop the correct position when defending 1vs1 and 2vs2 situations. With a 1vs1, the defender should look to press and push the attacker out wide, or get them on their weaker foot. In 2vs2s, one defender press the ball holder whilst the other should cover him and check the other attacker; the attackers will be looking to play between themselves, so anticipating this is good. Change the roles of players every so often.

Main part

A small-sided game, 4vs4, on a 40 x 30 m pitch with three small goals. Time 2 minutes x 4 repetitions per team.

Coaching

- Pressure on the player with the ball
- Diagonal coverage
- Compactness

- Communication (Me-You!)

Follow Up Session

A 10vs10 game in three zones for 2 x 8 minutes. Field 60 x 40 metres with two goalies. Players stay in their zones. Apply a 'ball-oriented' defence to each zone.

Coaching

Apply "ball-space" defence principles to each zone (defence-midfield-attack).

Defenders

- Overloads
- Press the ball holder
- Provide cover for your teammate
- Communication (talk between players: Me-You-Go-Stay-Cover)

Midfielders:

- Balance
- Press the ball holder
- Diagonal cover of teammates
- Close the opposition's space
- Don't allow short passes close to the ball holder… press and win the ball
- Develop a strong side (e.g. overload one side of the pitch, and outnumber the opposition, with players trying to win the ball back)

Attackers

- Underloads
- Press the ball holder
- Stay on the top of the triangle to support pressing players
- Don't allow short passes close to the ball holder… press and win the ball
- Develop a strong side (e.g. overload one side of the pitch, and outnumber the opposition, with players trying to win the ball back)

Follow Up Session II

Game, 11vs11 using the whole pitch. Apply "ball-space" defensive principles. Time 12 minutes.

Coaching

Apply the "ball-space" defensive principles that have been developed previously, in a real game. Emphasize line consistency and defensive transitions.

Recovery

6 minutes of slow running followed by 6 minutes of passive stretching.

Session 19 | Wednesday

Warm up

6 minutes of high energy stretching and running.

A passing game of 2 x 8 minutes using a passive defence. Field 60 x 70 metres (between the two penalty areas). Two teams of 10, change roles following a three minute break.

Coaching

The two teams of 10 players perform pre-determined moves; the attacking team should execute pre-planned offensive moves; the defending team should provide a passive "ball-space" defence. Change players' roles after 8 minutes. These zones have been created to develop the group's compactness when defending, as well as providing width when attacking (strong-weak side).

- Build up with small-medium passes
- Ensure players are positioned diagonally to offer support
- Do not allow big distances to emerge between the three lines

Attacking

- The four defenders have a maximum of two touches
- Encourage players to switch play to the other side of the pitch quickly
- Full backs support the attacking play
- Players should be very mobile; they need to create and find free areas
- One player should progress to the next zone (overloads)
- When completing an attack, players should try one-two passes to penetrate the defence

Defending (passive)

- Do not allow big distances to develop between the defenders
- Press the player with ball
- Check near passing options

- Take up diagonal positions
- Communicate (Me-You, Go-Close)

Main part

20 minutes of aggressive shadow game play, with pre-determined passing and combinations, and direction from the coach (with two independent teams). Focus on three to four different attacking (build-up) moves and conduct multiple repetitions to embed the learning. All the players participate in all the moves and positions, relative to the ball, until the end of the phase. Both groups should practice simultaneously. Each repetition starts from a set position for all the players, and a pass from the goalkeeper.

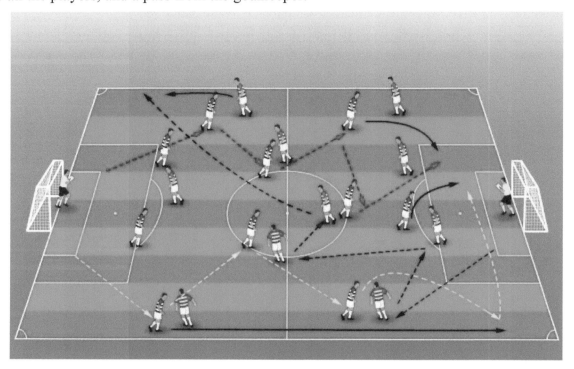

Coaching

1. Full backs provide attacking support
2. Defensive midfielders swap sides
3. Encourage vertical passes to attacker(s) furthest up the pitch

Follow Up Session

An 11vs11 game across the entire pitch. 2 x 12 minutes.

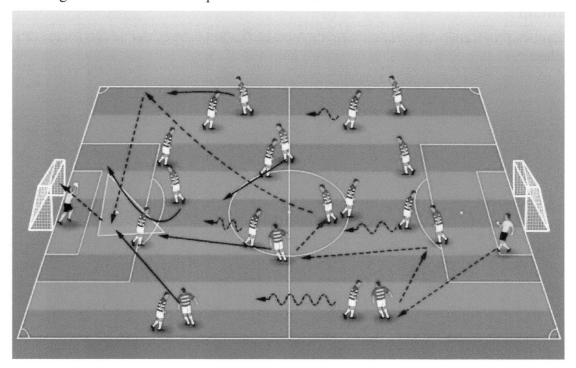

Coaching

This is a real game implementation of the movements that were worked on during the previous practice.

Provide individual player evaluations and guidance during the break, and at the end of the game.

Recovery

6 minutes of slow running then 4 minutes of passive stretching.

Session 20 | Thursday (morning)

Warm up

6 minutes of high energy exercises then 8 minutes of technique practice in subgroups of six to ten players.

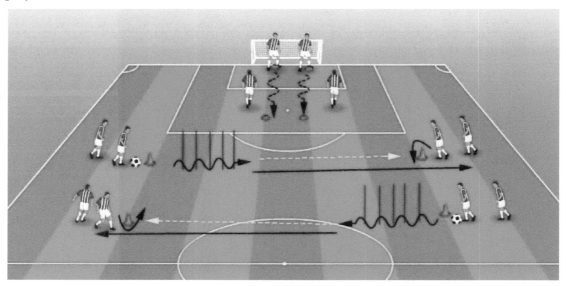

Across two stations, focus on passing-dribbling drills.

Main part

Power exercises for 30 seconds across 10 stations. 30 minutes total time.

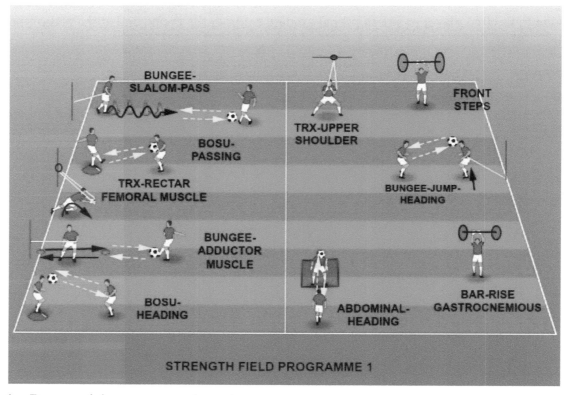

1. Bungee slalom moves and passing
2. Bosu skipping and passing with foot changes
3. TRX exercise for femoral muscle
4. Bungee side-steps and passing
5. Bosu skipping and heading

6. Abdominals heading
7. Foot-rises with a bar
8. Bungee-jump-heading
9. Bar front steps
10. TRX upperzone

After each exercise, each player has to run, at speed, for 10 m then jump (as if for a header) at the end, before beginning the next exercise.

Follow Up Session

Pro-speed drill (preparing for speed training). Six repetitions with a full break between each.

Preparing the players for speed training. Eight stations of 20 m each:

1. Rhythmic jumps alternate
2. Skating (ladder steps)
3. Sneaks
4. Change direction speed
5. Reverse steps (backwards)
6. Two Rotational turns
7. Diagonal jumps on one leg
8. Sprint 20 m

All the drills should be executed with maximum commitment and speed.

Recovery

8 minutes of slow running followed by 6 minutes of stretching.

Warm up

A 12 minute passing drill in two subgroups. Utilise an attacking zone and a defending zone.

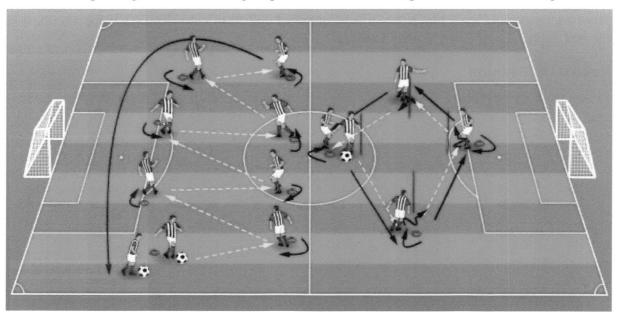

The defenders and midfielders engage in the passing drill, whilst the attackers complete their own diamond passing move. Pass and follow.

Emphasize pass quality, feints, body position, and being in position to receive the next ball.

Finally, utilize 8 minutes of movement and dynamic stretching.

Main part

20 minutes of attacking moves in subgroups of four (shadow game).

The midfielder makes a vertical pass to the attacker who makes a wall pass to a midfielder in diagonal space. The player who makes the final pass into the penalty area has three player options, for passing the ball. The three potential receiving players make a triangle in the penalty area to cover the space in 3 different places for the attempt on goal.

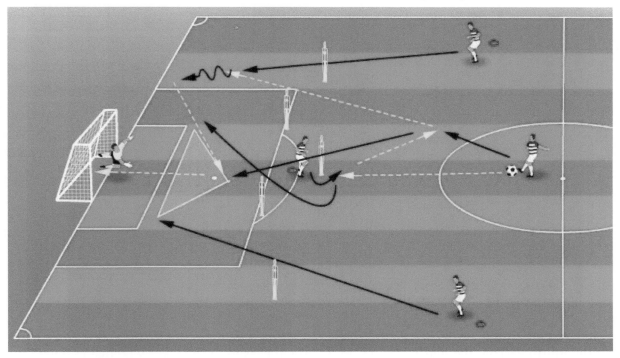

In a second variant (below), the midfielder makes a vertical pass to the attacker who makes a wall pass back to the midfielder who makes a long pass to a wide attacker (or full back) for a cross into the penalty area. Attackers should, once again, create a triangle.

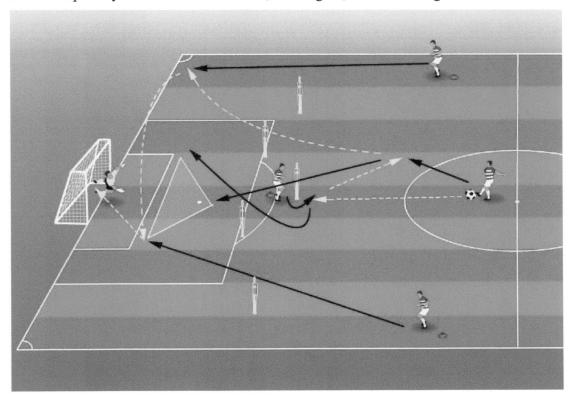

In the third variant, the midfielder makes a vertical pass to the attacker who makes a wall pass back to the midfielder who makes a long pass in the other side of the pitch. The aim here he is to change the direction of play to the weaker side. For the final phase – the shot on goal – the attackers should, once again, create a triangle.

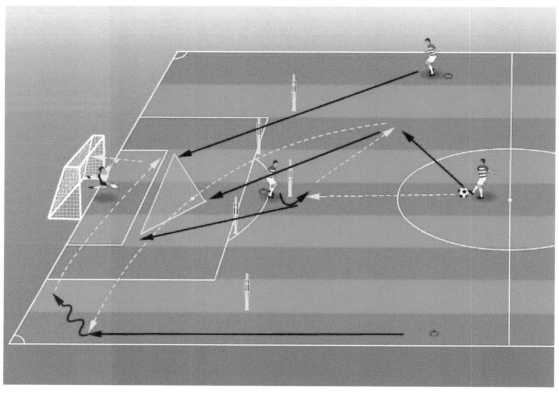

In the fourth variant, the midfielder makes a vertical pass to the attacker who makes a wall pass backwards. Then we have a pass between the defenders (the mannequins) for an attacker who moves in behind the defenders (mannequins) to receive the ball.

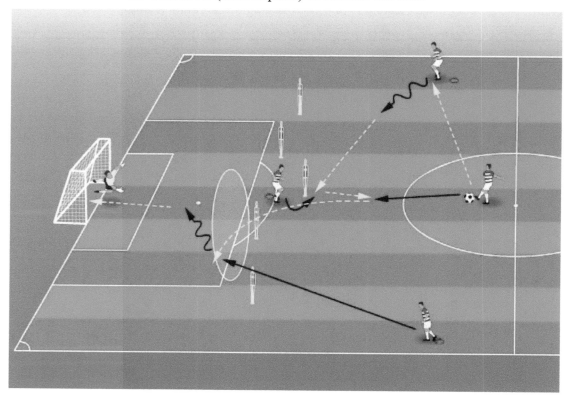

Follow Up Session

A 12 minute game. Repeat the previous exercises (above) but use two (possibly three) real defenders.

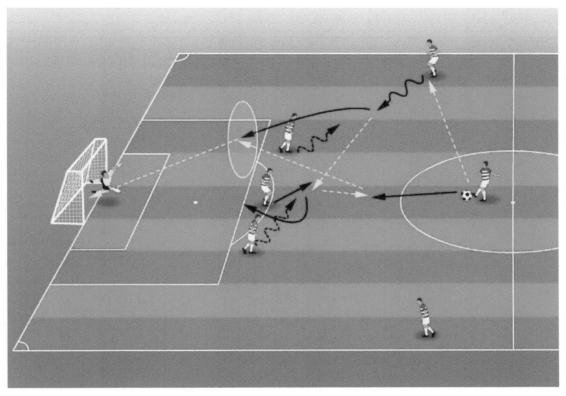

Use offside rules.

Follow Up Session II

A 9 minute running drill comprising of 30 seconds of fast running followed by 30 seconds of slow running in three subgroups.

Recovery

8 minutes of passive stretching.

Session 22 | Friday

Warm up

6 minutes of active stretching and running exercises.

A 14 minute rondo game, 5vs2, on an 8 x 8 m pitch. This is a transition game; when the two defenders win the ball, they change the game (e.g. pass the ball on to the next rondo group). Then they follow their pass and start a new rondo game.

As a variant, for every field change, move three different players.

Main part

A 10 minute shooting drill (Inverted "T"). Players move as shown. One player shoots from the left, one shoots from the right.

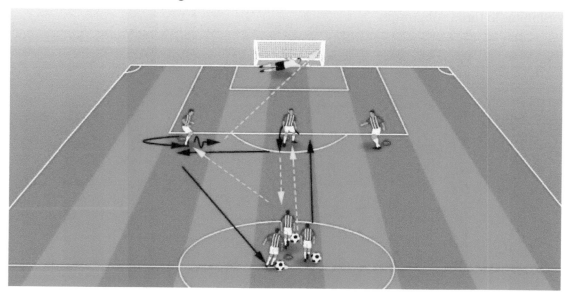

Coaching

Pass and follow. One from the left, one from the right.

Coaches should be looking for:

- Clean passing
- Good receipt of the ball
- Shots into the opposite corners of the goal
- Forward movement before receiving the ball

Follow Up Session

20 minutes of set pieces (corner kicks).

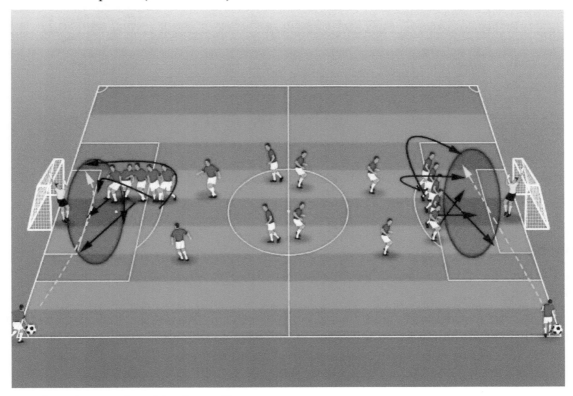

1. Five players placed horizontally
2. Five players placed vertically

Coaching

The positioning of the incoming ball is directed with a signal. The ball is delivered accordingly, irrespective of where the players are, into the area. The players must move to specific points on the pitch, regardless of where the ball is directed.

Follow Up Session II

Defenders are added.

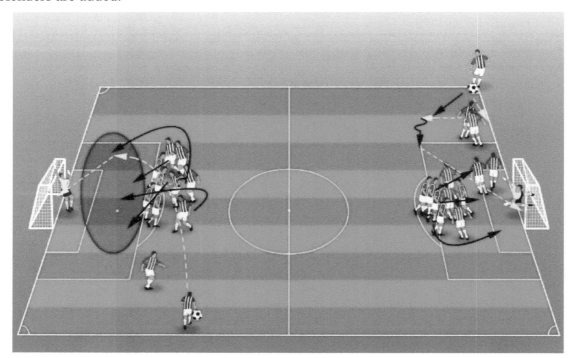

1. Free kicks from the side
2. Double pass, then a shot on goal

Coaching

Use two players, close to each other (like a short corner), to create an overload before shooting on goal.

Assign players, in the penalty area, whose job is to move in front of the goalkeeper and make it more difficult for him to save the ball.

Follow Up Session III

8 minutes of crossing and finishing in subgroups of three players.

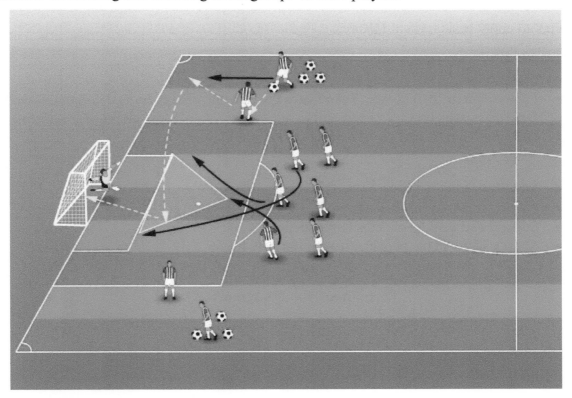

Coaching

The three attacking players' movements should be pre-determined. Watch the two players on the side. Players should sprint in at the moment of crossing.

The crossing should be forceful (no slow, drifting crosses here!).

The crossed ball should curl away from the goalkeeper.

Recovery

6 minutes of slow running followed by 6 minutes of stretching.

Session 23 | Saturday

A friendly 90 minutes match (60 minutes for 1st XI players; 30 minutes for 2nd XI players)

Attempt to apply basic tactical features.

Defensive function:

- Closed lines
- Pressure on the ball holder (Teammates provide diagonal cover and communicate!)
- Defensive transition
- Defending on the halfway line (high up the pitch)

Attacking function:

- Mobility and movement, on and off the ball
- Staying wide to create space
- Support and help teammates in possession
- Three players in the penalty area for the final phase

Formations 1-4-2-3-1 and 1-4-3-3

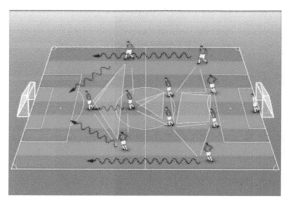 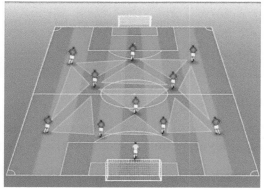

Implement the set pieces that have been developed in training.

When the opposition are dispossessed, fast counter-attacking is a priority.

Day 21 | Sunday | Rest

Week 4

MONDAY	TUESDAY	WEDNESDAY	THURSDAY	FRIDAY	SATURDAY	SUNDAY
SOCCER POWER	SPECIAL SOCCER ENDURANCE	SOCCER POWER	SPECIAL SOCCER ENDURANCE	SOCCER POWER	FRIENDLY MATCH	REST
BASIC SOCCER ENDURANCE	TACTICS	BASIC SOCCER ENDURANCE	TACTICS	SPEED		
				BASIC SOCCER ENDURANCE		
TACTICS		TACTICS		TACTICS		

The fourth week has three more morning sessions, with strength, speed, and power-speed (soccer power) elements. We begin, through small sided games, to train football endurance with appropriate players. We also seek cooperation with our line formations (e.g. cooperation of the defensive line (between defenders); cooperation of the midfield line, etc.). These lines can be seen as sub-units of the overall team. Basic strength, coordination, and speed with the ball, are in our session plans too.

In week 4, the primary focus is on training and improving defensive behavior and line co-operation. We will continue training set pieces at the end of the week. On Saturday, we have our fourth friendly game, and we shall use players in the same 60 minute, 30 minute split, as done previously. Those who we intend to be key players will have more game time.

Warm up

6 minutes of running stretching exercises, followed by 10 minutes of passing technique in pairs.

Power exercises. 30 seconds at each of the 10 stations, for 30 minutes.

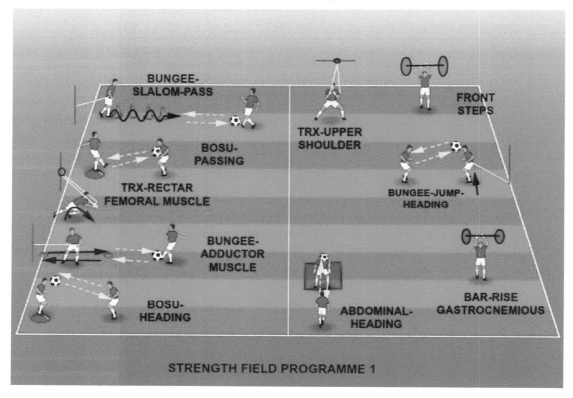

STRENGTH FIELD PROGRAMME 1

1. Bungee slalom moves and passing
2. Bosu skipping and passing with foot changes
3. TRX exercise for femoral muscle
4. Bungee side-steps and passing
5. Bosu heading
6. Abdominals heading
7. Foot-rises with a bar; lift the edge of the foot up and down
8. Bungee-jump-heading
9. Bar front steps; switch the front foot
10. TRX upperzone

After each exercise, each player has to run, at speed, for 12 m, before moving to the next station.

Main part

Speed training. Four soccer speed exercises, by Chr. Mourikis, with four repetitions per exercise.

Exercise 1 (bottom exercise): Slow running to the partner, followed by a sprint. The partner tries to catch up for 15m.

Exercise 2: Slow movement to the defender before a pass right or left into the diagonal space. The attacking player must turn and control the ball before the cone before turning back, passing the ball to the defender, and sprinting 15 m.

Exercise 3: High skipping for 5 m; low skipping for 5 m, slalom, sprint 15m

Exercise 4 (top exercise): Skipping followed by a back pass; then a turn with 4 jumps followed by a sprint of 15 m. The player low skips for 3 seconds then plays a wall-pass with their partner; then, they must turn and do four cone jumps (40 cm) before sprinting 15 m with a ball (dribbling).

Recovery

8 minutes of slow running followed by 6 minutes of passive stretching.

Session 25 | Monday (afternoon)

Warm up

6 minutes of high energy running exercises.

2 x 8 minute passing game with a passive defence. Field 60 x 70 m. Change roles in the middle. Break for 3 minutes.

Coaching

The two teams of 10 players are playing a passing game. One team keeps the ball and the other offers a passive defence, based on defensive principles. Change the roles for the second 8 minute period. Zones have been created to facilitate the group's compactness when defending.

Development Movements:
- Move the ball from side to side away from the four defenders (weak side)
- Alternate defensive midfielders; have the other midfielders provide support to the attackers
- Look to have wider attackers co-operating with No 9 and No 10, for 1-2 passes or passes down the middle

Main part

A 10 minute drill for pressuring the ball holder. Three x 3 minutes (break for 1 minute at the end of each period). Area 30 x 30 m. Change roles on the break. The four players in the middle zone try to cut out the pass from the right-hand team to the left-hand team (and back) and, as every ball is passed, create a new defensive line.

When the ball is in the middle of the park, the defenders should take up diagonal positions, close to each other, to make a defensive triangle. Do not allow the ball to pass!

When the ball is at the side of the pitch, two defenders create a diagonal position (one presses the ball holder, one covers their teammate) and the other two come close and create a line.

Coaching

Players can only move in their zones. The middle group defends, and their focus is on the ball holder. The ball is moved from player to player in the outer zones, with a minimum of two contacts. After 5-6 changes, they must pass to the opposite outer zone/team (ground passes only), between defenders.

- Diagonal cover of teammate
- Compactness
- Communication between defenders

Follow Up Session

Small-sided tactical game 7vs7 (up to 9vs9) in a 60 x 70 m space. The emphasis is on defensive work. Time 20 minutes.

Coaching

- Defending space principles
- The consistency of defensive lines
- Holding a defensive line, 5-6 metres outside the penalty area
- The goalkeeper participates in the defensive work, providing exits/cover on vertical passes behind the defenders

Recovery

6 minutes of slow running followed by 6 minutes of stretching.

Warm up

6 minutes of high energy running exercises

14 minutes of working with the ball in two subgroups

In two squares of 10 x 10 m, with scattered cones; players dribble with balls whilst avoiding cones and teammates. The other subgroup runs coordination exercises around the perimeter. Time of 6 minutes (2 x 3 minutes with role changes during a 1 minute break).

Main part

Special endurance in small-sided games 3vs3 (4vs4), on a small pitch of 20 x 30 m. Three parallel matches of 8 minutes (4 minutes each half, 2 minute break). All players do each game.

1. Two goals in a 5 x 2 m space with an emphasis on collaboration and the creation/execution of shots on goal
2. 1vs1 situations, emphasizing individual defensive and offensive tactics
3. Using four small goals that rapidly change the thinking and direction of the game

Follow Up Session

An 8 minute running drill of 7 seconds sprinting, then 53 seconds of slow running, repeated.

Recovery

6 minutes of slow running followed by 6 minutes of passive stretching.

Warm up

6 minutes of active stretching

12 minutes of ball work and general coordination work

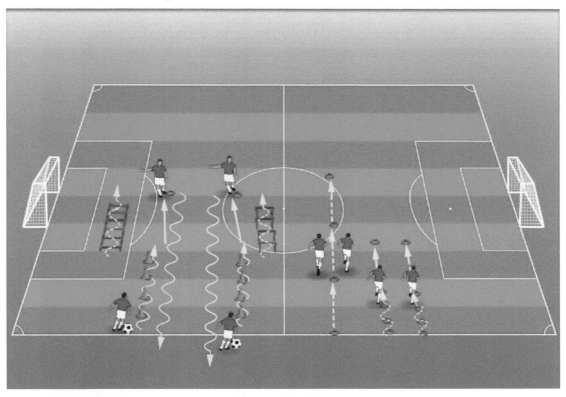

Slalom moves, passing, dribbling, coordination drills. 2 sets of 5 minutes.

Main part

30 metres of sprinting with an increase in speed every 10 m. (60-80-100%) - 4 repetitions.

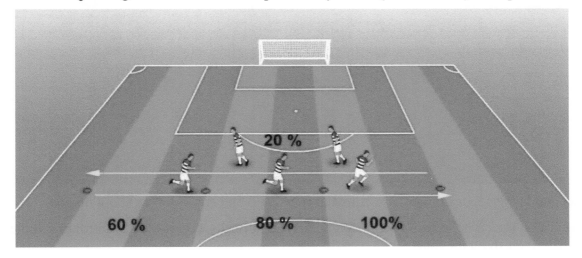

Follow Up Session

5 metres of skipping, followed by 10 meters of sprinting, repeated 6 times.

Follow Up Session II

Speed with a ball: Three exercises of 6 repetitions.

Exercise 1: Pass to teammate, use elliptical speed and ball control, then shoot on goal.

Exercise 2: Receive the ball, fake a shot on goal, elliptical speed and ball control to dribble the ball, then shoot on goal.

Exercise 3: Sprint 4 m with three changes of direction, receive the ball, fake a shot on goal, then dribble the ball around the mannequin, and shoot on goal.

Recovery

8 minutes of slow running followed by 5 minutes of passive stretching.

Session 28 | Wednesday (afternoon)

Warm up

8 minutes updating players on the purpose of your training. Use a tactics board.

Fundamentals:

- Pressure on the ball holder
- Cut out crossing options
- Maintain the correct distances between players
- Stay consistent
- Communicate

Warm up II

6 minutes of active stretching and running.

Warm up III

An 8 minute game on half the field, 8vs8. Blues try to keep the ball, reds try to tackle them. Passive defending only.

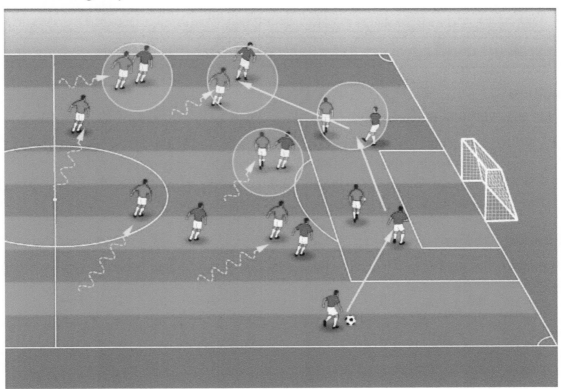

77

Main part

10 minutes of orientation. Coaches will coach the team in possession of the ball. You are developing solutions for "breaking" and relieving opposition pressure.

Coaching

Provide solutions to reduce opposition pressure:

1. With coordinated movements from the defensive midfielder and a wide midfielder, pass the ball behind the opposition to force them to turn (two options)
2. With the support of the defensive midfielder, get the central defenders to move the ball to the less defended side of the pitch

Follow Up Session

A 10 minute learning phase. Coach the team which is trying to gain possession. Show them solutions and positioning.

Solution 1: the ball is with a central defender:

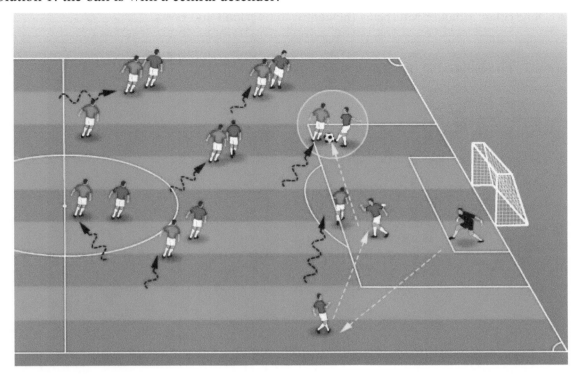

- One attacker presses, the other closes down the passing option to the other central defender
- The wide midfielder closes down the option to a wide defender
- The defensive midfielder who asks for the ball gets pressed

Solution 2: The ball to a wide defender

- The wide midfielder presses
- The attacker, on the inside, closes down the option for a backpass to the central defender
- Our wide defender pushes up to the midfielder to prevent a pass

- The defensive midfielder is squeezed by the central midfielder
- The other attacker returns to the centre to overload and press

Solution 3: The ball to the defensive midfielder

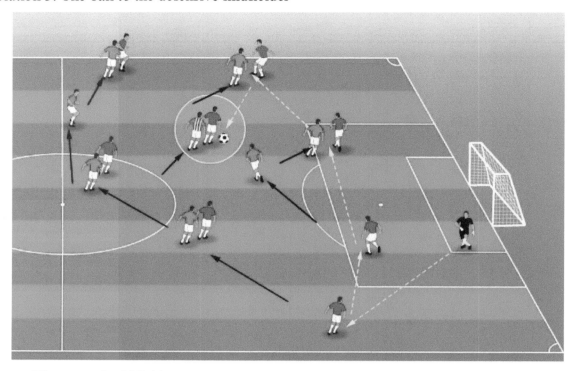

- The central midfielder presses
- The wide fullback and the other wide midfielder close down passing options (forming a defensive triangle)
- The onside attacker returns for an overload

Solution 4: Changing sides

- The wide midfielder returns to cover press
- The group shifts diagonally, towards the ball to provide support
- Create defensive depth

4 minutes of feedback.

Follow Up Session II

20 minutes of applying what has just been trained, in a full game, in a 60 x 80 m space.

5 minutes of training evaluation.

Recovery

6 minutes of slow running, followed by 6 minutes of stretching.

Warm up

6 minutes of energetic stretching in the area, together with the coach

12 minutes of exercises that develop coordination, in two subgroups. Area 20 m x 20 m.

The players (in pairs) start together, one dribbling with a ball, the other without. In the middle, change the ball holder (step); the non-ball holder now jumps using the ladder, whilst the other dribbles the ball. The players change roles in every repeat.

Main part

Small-sided games, 5vs5, in a space of 45 x 25 m., with subgroups comprised of two lines (e.g. 4 defenders and 1 defensive midfielder; or 2 defensive midfielders and 3 attackers; or 1 central attacker, 3 midfielders, and 1 defensive midfielder).

These small-sided games have lots of pressing! Formation-based use of players. The aim here is to develop special soccer endurance and tactical improvement. Time 5 minutes x 2 halves x 2 sets. Break for 1 minute per game, and 4 minutes between the sets.

Emphasis on:

Attack: Mobility, cooperation, transitions, and the final attempts on goal.

Defence: Pressing the ball holder, providing cover, transitions, and communication.

Follow Up Session

12 minutes of set pieces: throw-ins.

Two variants:

1. Two players are in the penalty area looking to receive the ball. The first leaves the ball and turns to receive the ball from the second player. Then he can a) shoot on goal or b) pass to a teammate outside the penalty area for a shot (left on the figure).
2. One player moves to the ball holder and another runs behind him into free space. This second player receives the ball and crosses (long pass) into the penalty area for the attackers (right on the figure).

Recovery

8 minutes of slow running followed by 6 minutes of passive stretching.

Session 30 | Friday (morning)

Warm up

6 minutes of running and stretching exercises, then 8 minutes of pair-based exercises to develop technique.

Main part

Power exercises. 30 seconds per station, across 10 stations. Two sets totalling 40 minutes.

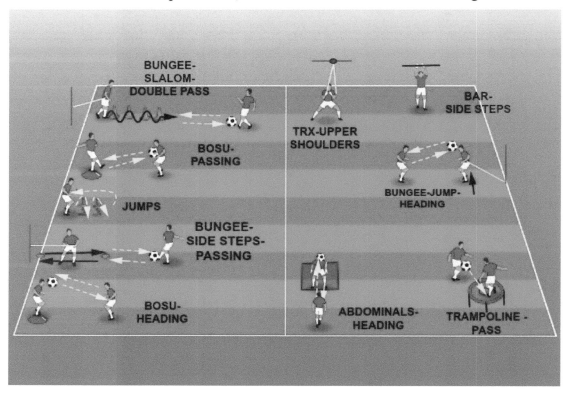

1. Bungee slalom moves and passing
2. Bosu skipping and passing with foot changes
3. Continuous jumping
4. Bungee side-steps and passing
5. Bosu skipping and heading
6. Abdominals heading
7. Trampoline passing
8. Bungee-jump-heading
9. Bar side steps
10. TRX – upper zone

After each exercise, the player does a 10 m speed run with a change of direction.

Recovery

6 minutes of running followed by 6 minutes of stretching.

Session 31 | Friday (afternoon)

Warm up

6 minutes of active stretching in running drills.

A 14 minute passing game (using hands only) in the penalty area where the ball must be kept off the ground. (4 minutes x 3 sets with 1 minute breaks). The three sets should be broken down into: 1. Movement and shot on goal in 10 passes); 2. goal attempts with headers; 3. goal attempts with shots.

Main part

Reaction speed 6 metres x 6 repetitions x 2 sets.

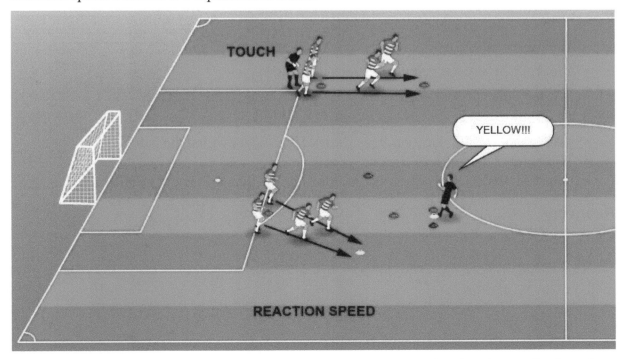

Sprint to 3 colours over 6 m. The coach steps on a colour to give the signal, or calls the colour aloud. 2. In another group, the trainer touches the shoulder of a player who reacts with a 6 metre sprint. A player standing by the side of the player tries to sprint and overtake the first player but can only 'go' when the first player starts his run.

Follow Up Session

Set piece practice (corner kicks). We use defenders this time. Two teams 11vs11.

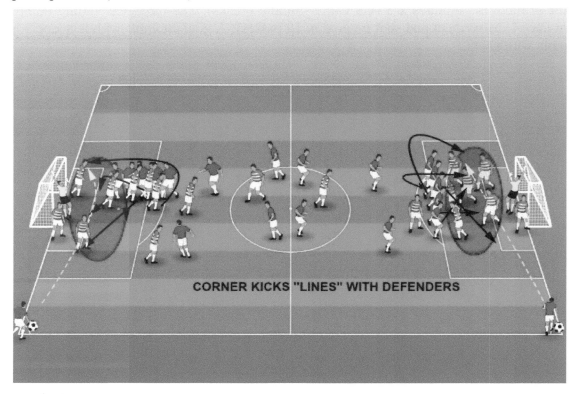

CORNER KICKS "LINES" WITH DEFENDERS

Two variants:

1. Five players placed horizontally in the penalty area (right on figure)
2. Five players placed vertically in the penalty area (left on figure)

Coaching

The player taking the corner:

- Specifies where the ball will be delivered (signal)
- Delivers the ball *after* the initial movement of players in the area

Players:

- Move to a specific location, regardless of who is delivering the ball
- Do not stop trying, until the play is complete
- Use 1-2 players, as decoys, to "free" the players who are best at heading

Recovery

8 minutes of slow running followed by 6 minutes of stretching.

Friendly Match

Match time 60 minutes for the 1st XI players, and 30 minutes for the 2nd XI players
Attempt to apply general basic tactical features:

Defensive functions:

1. Create a high line up the pitch, 10 meters in front of the center line
2. Pressure on the ball holder, teammate diagonal cover, and communication!
3. Balance when creating a defensive overload
4. Reaction to loose balls – effective defensive transitions

Attacking functions:

1. Good mobility and movement, on and off the ball
2. Staying wide to create space
3. Supporting and helping teammates in possession
4. Attempts on goal are a priority

Formations 1-4-2-3-1 and 1-4-4-2

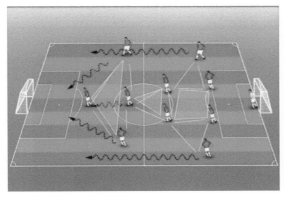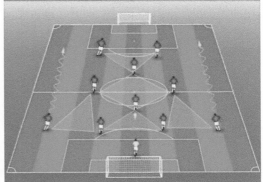

"Ball-based" spatial defence!

In 1-4-2-3-1:

- The three players around "No 9" change their positions
- Those three players also move to find space at the back of the defence

In the 1-4-4-2 formation:

- The two strikers move the defence around (one goes for the ball, one moves into space; or they crisscross, etc.
- The # 10 (central midfielder) comes into the penalty area from behind, moving behind the two attackers, trying to escape the attention of defenders
- Vertical passing options between lines should be opened up
- The two wide midfielders should come in and provide shots on goal

Day 28 | Sunday | Rest

Week 5

MONDAY	TUESDAY	WEDNESDAY	THURSDAY	FRIDAY	SATURDAY	SUNDAY
BASIC SOCCER ENDURANCE	SPEED	SPECIAL SOCCER ENDURANCE	SOCCER SPEED	SPECIAL SOCCER ENDURANCE	FRIENDLY MATCH	REST
TACTICS	SOCCER SPEED	TACTICS	BASIC SOCCER ENDURANCE	TACTICS		
	BASIC SOCCER ENDURANCE					
	TACTICS		TACTICS			

For the fifth week, we focus on special strength training, through small-sided games; we also include the last two morning (double) sessions.

This week, there is a focus on the cooperation of players in holding their lines, with the appropriate separation between players (3-4 offensive, defensive, midfielders). We also focus on the team's offensive and defensive tactics, defensive cooperation, and aggression in the attacking half. We'll cover the training and coaching of two formations that you will use (1-4-2-3-1 and 1-4-3-3). For set plays, we'll look to develop corners and free kicks.

In the fifth friendly game, we use the players as they would be used in a normal league game. Our substitutions are dictated by the needs of the game.

Warm up

6 minutes of active stretching as directed by the coach.

A 2 x 8 minute passing game with a passive defence. Area 60 x 70 m. Rotate groups every 8 minutes, and break for 3 minutes.

Coaching

Two teams of 10 players have a passing game. Use pre-planned attacking plays, and a passive defence which uses defence-oriented space on the ball. The players change roles every 8 minutes. Zones should be utilised to facilitate the compactness of the group when defending. Zones also help players to create space (in terms of width and depth) when they have to build up play. Four ways to build-up (attacking) collaborations are:

- Add another player on defence to challenge the opposition further
- Generate overloads from the midfielder who looks for free space in the centre of the pitch
- Employ a "hidden" attacker move, by the offensive midfielder (10)
- Wide attackers should move infield to free up space for the full-backs

Main part

20 minutes of attacking build-up without any active interactions from the opposition (shadow game), with pre-designed moves and clear direction from the coach. All the players should participate until the end of the period. Each cycle starts with the ball being placed on the ground by the goalkeeper and passed.

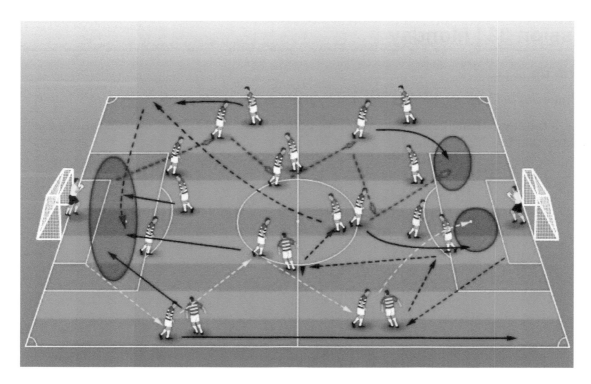

Coaching

1. Use full-backs in build-ups and attacking overloads with quick changes of direction (move the ball from right to left, or left to right)
2. Kick-off by a wide midfielder
3. Vertical pass for wide attacker, then a back-pass to a midfielder who comes into the penalty area
4. The hidden player 'holds' behind an attacker

Follow Up Session

A 12 minute game, 11vs11, across the whole field, implementing everything learned in the previous session.

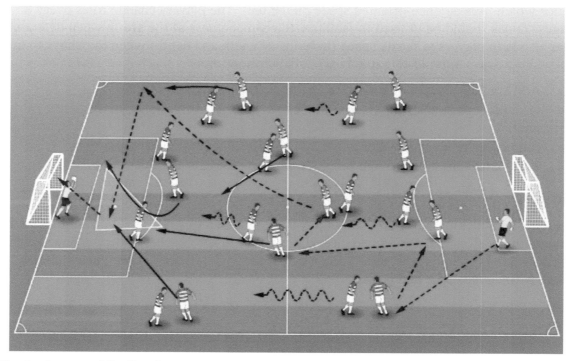

Offer 4 minutes of feedback.

Follow Up Session II

A 9 minute running drill in 30 second (sprint) – 30 second (slow) form, in three subgroups.

Recovery

4 minutes of slow running followed by 6 minutes of passive stretching.

Warm up

6 minutes of energetic stretching and running.

12 minutes of passing drills in a 1-4-2-3-1 formation. Carry out two x 6 minute periods, with a change of direction for the second period.

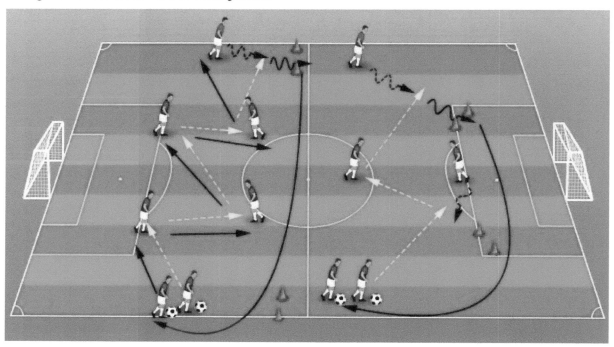

Pass and follow. The last player dribbles to the start. Focus on quality passing and body positions.

Main part

A running exercise, at speed, for 30 m with an increase in speed every 10 m. Six repetitions.

Another group of players does 5 m of skipping then 5 m of sprinting. Six repetitions.

All players do both exercises.

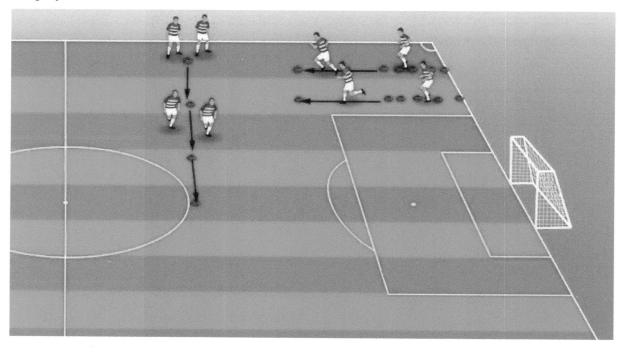

Follow Up Session

Soccer speed and power with shots on goal: four exercises of 4 repetitions.

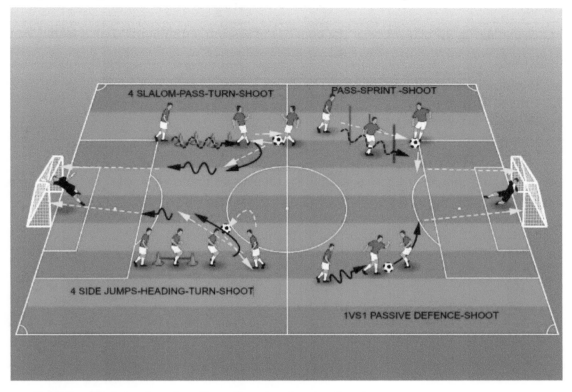

- Drill 1: side jumping, heading, then turning to shoot
- Drill 2: dribbling then shooting
- Drill 3: passing, then slaloming through poles, then instant shooting
- Drill 4: slaloming through cones, passing, then turning and shooting

Recovery

8 minutes of slow, lazy, running followed by 6 minutes of passive stretching.

Warm up

8 minutes explaining to players what the goal of the session's training is. Use a tactics board.

Fundamentals:

1. Pressure on the ball holder
2. Cross-field coverage
3. Distance between players
4. Compactness of lines
5. Communication

Follow this with 6 minutes of active stretching, then an 8 minute game of 6 vs 6. Play on half the pitch, with a passive defence, and three small goals on the centre line.

Main part

10 minutes of orientation; teach the defending team to close space and provide support options to defenders.

Coaching

1. Apply pressure on the wide defender
2. Close any back pass options for the central defender
3. Apply pressure on the defensive midfielder
4. Check the opposite central defender

Follow Up Session

10 minutes of guided learning. Coach the team to come up with effective solutions and positioning.

Solution 1: Move the ball quickly to the free wide defender.

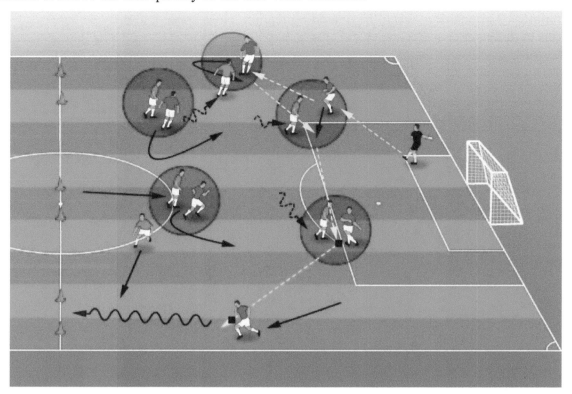

Solution 2: The midfielder peels back, enabling a pass to be played behind the back line.

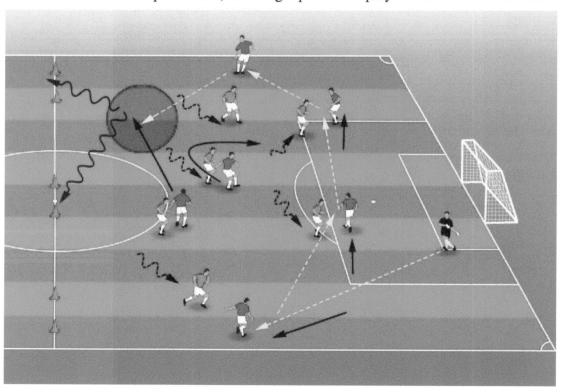

Solution 3: Holding full back with a change of side from the defensive midfielder.

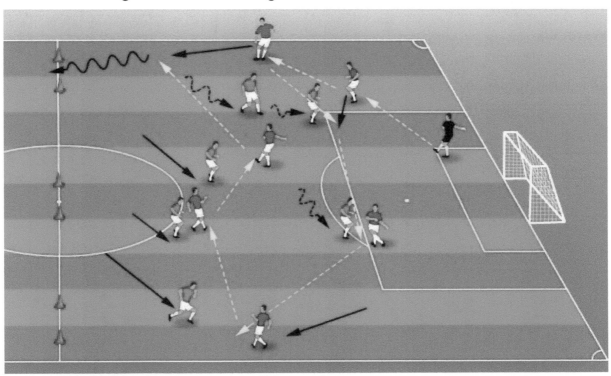

Follow up the on field training with 4 minutes of feedback.

Follow Up Session II

A 20 minute final game on a 60 x 80 m pitch. 8vs8.

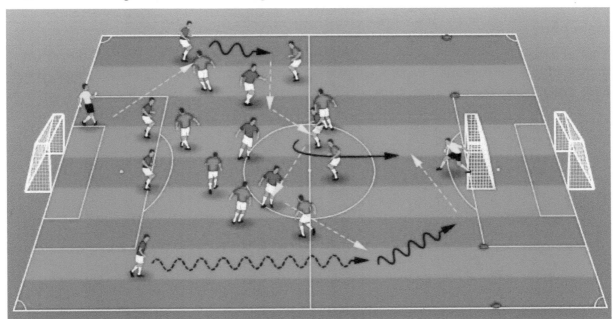

Use the three solutions, just developed, in a real game. Provide three minutes of evaluation once the game has finished.

Recovery

6 minutes of slow running followed by 6 minutes of stretching.

Warm up

6 minutes of active stretching.

14 minutes of coordinated passing drills in two subgroups.

The two subgroups change roles every 6 minutes with a 1 minute break in-between. The players develop passing variations and have four different agility stations.

Main part

Special soccer endurance through small-sided games. The playing space is 30 × 20 m. Three games, played for 4 minutes each. Each player must take part in two sets of each game. Break after every game.

- Bottom game: Normal goals with keepers; the emphasis is on finishing phases
- Middle game: 1 goal for training 1vs1 situations
- Top game: 4 small goals for developing changes in the direction of play

Follow Up Session

A running drill in a diagonal pattern, alternating forwards and backwards. Six repetitions.

Recovery

8 minutes of slow running followed by 6 minutes of passive stretching.

Warm up

6 minutes of active running and stretching.

12 minutes of coordinated activities, with balls, in two subgroups. Time 2 x 6 minutes.

One team is in the middle of the pitch, dribbling. The other is on the side, completing agility and passing-heading moves.

Main part

Special Soccer Power:

1. Two drills without ball (2 x 4 reps)
2. Formation 1-4-2-3-1 based drill 4 vs 2 (8 reps)

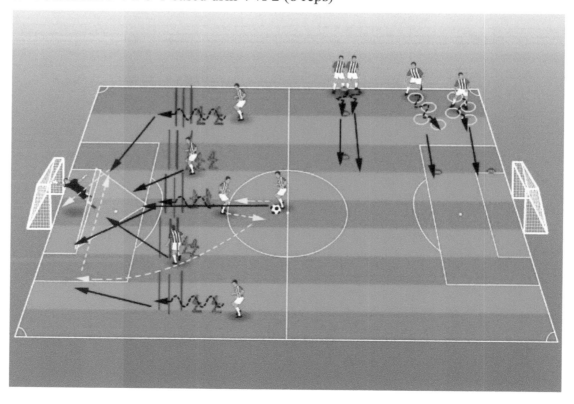

For the side drills:

1. Two players push against each other's shoulders for about 5 m. Then, they run at speed for 15 m
2. Each player jumps on their right foot 4 times, then on their left. Then runs at speed for 15 m

For the main drill:

1. 4 vs 2 with kick-off in the centre circle. Each player has 2 jumps, 3 slaloms, and a burst of speed. The attackers create an aggressive triangle in the penalty area, where we have a 3 vs 2 situation

Emphasis on:

1. Quality of the final cross or pass
2. Avoiding the opposition
3. Creating the right finishes on goal
4. Covering space and the reaction of defensive players

Follow Up Session

A tactical game on the whole pitch. Formations 1-4-2-3-1 vs 1-4-3-3. Time 20 minutes.

Coaching

A counter attacking game. Play always starts from a corner kick. After the corner kick, players play a regular game until the ball goes dead, or the coach stops the game for a new corner kick. Also the coach can add a second ball to create sudden transition situations. All the players must focus on the second ball! This variation will help develop counter attacks and transitions.

Recovery

8 minutes of slow running followed by 4 minutes of stretching.

Warm up

6 minutes of energetic stretching in pairs.

A 14 minute passing game, using hands, in the penalty area. Time 4 minutes x 3 sets with a 1 minute break per game.

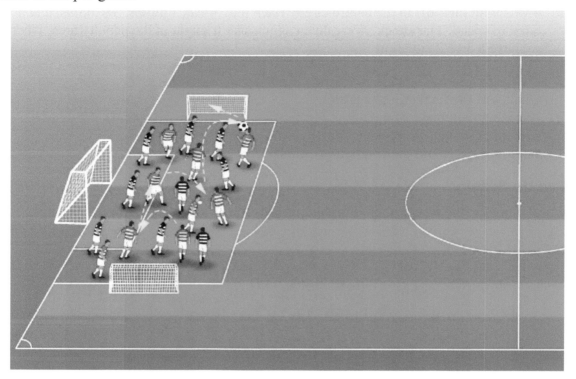

Game variations:

1. Simple passing – a goal must be scored in 10 passes or less
2. A goal can only be scored with a header
3. Shots on goal are feet-only

Main part

Speed drill 10 m x 8 sets.

Follow Up Session

1-4-3-3 vs 1-4-4-2 formations. Playing two systems to highlight advantages and disadvantages.

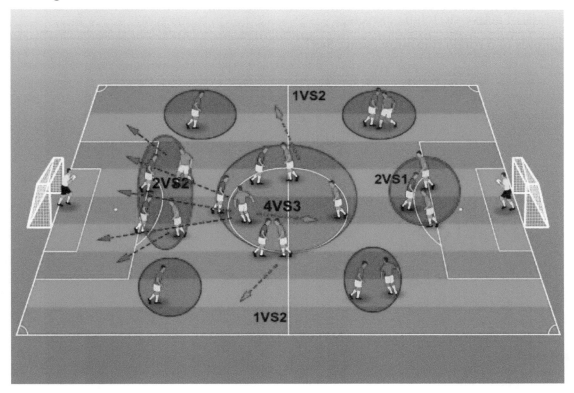

Coaching

1-4-3-3: Offensive exploitation of full-backs and cooperation with wide attackers for overloads. In defence, the wide defenders need to stay compact.

1-4-4-2: Exploitation of the free centre back, holding the overload in the centre, and the ball in for the 'No 9' (for 2vs2 + 1). In defence, take care of the full-back (central midfielder returns with opening of inside midfielder).

4 minutes of feedback.

Recovery

6 minutes of slow running and 6 minutes of passive stretching.

Warm up

6 minutes of active stretching exercises.

14 minutes of a rondo transition game; 5vs2.

Main part

Reaction speed exercise.

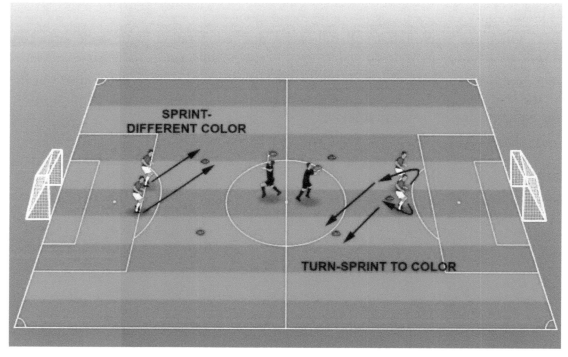

- Drill 1: In pairs, react to the direction of the coach (sprint to different coloured cones, as instructed) 8 m x 6 repetitions
- Drill 2: In pairs, signal-turn-sprint to the called cone. 8 m x 6 repetitions

Follow Up Session

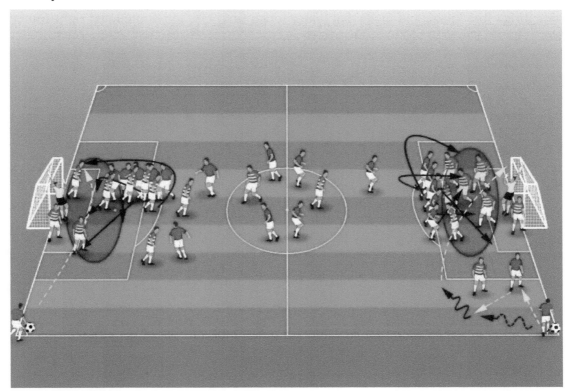

1. Corner kick

- An attacker goes to the near post
- An attacker goes to the far post
- Passing for 2vs1 in the corner, followed by a shot on goal. Everyone moves to crowd the goalie!

Use two teams in each half of the field. Play until a goal is scored or the coach stops things.

2. Wide kick-off

3. Free kicks

Practice direct free kicks, and kicks that take a touch first. Use left-footed and right-footed players.

4. Throw-ins

- Combined movements in the penalty area to create conditions conducive to an attempt on goal
- Opposite movement to the side, to create conditions for a cross into the penalty box

Recovery

6 minutes of slow running followed by 6 minutes of stretching.

Session 40 | Saturday | Friendly match

A championship approach for the players. Make substitutions, in relation to the needs of the game, but ensure that enough players get game time.

Treat the game, like a normal League game.

In defence

- Hold the defensive line 10 m ahead of the centre line!
- Pressure the ball holder
- Offer teammates diagonal cover
- Communicate!
- Create balance in any defensive-overload
- React when the ball is loose!
- Perform effective defensive transitions.
- Have an emphasis on 1vs1 where fighters are winners!

In attack

- Mobility; lots of movement both on and off the ball
- Stay wide to create space
- Support teammates in possession
- Shooting is a priority

Formation 1-4-2-3-1

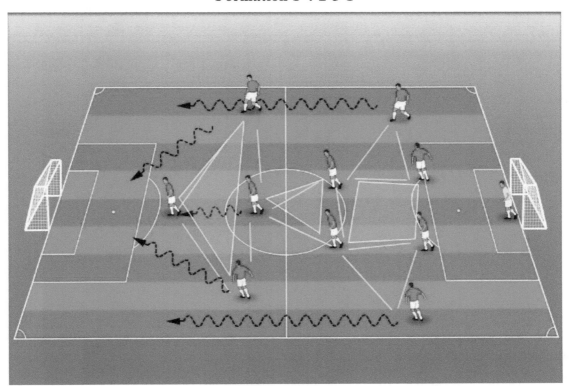

- "Ball based" spatial defence!
- In 1-4-2-3-1, the three players behind the 'No 9' change their positions
- Those three players also move to find space behind the opposition defence
- Full backs exploit space

Defensive organization in static phases

Defensive corner-kicks: one player at the near post, one free in the area, one on the edge of the penalty area, two players close to the centre-line for counter attacks.

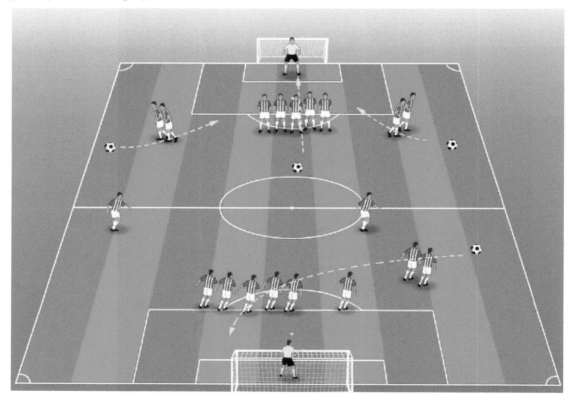

Wide kicks: 2 players make a "wall".

A defensive line is formed on the penalty area's line.

Sunday | Rest

Week 6

MONDAY	TUESDAY	WEDNESDAY	THURSDAY	FRIDAY	SATURDAY	SUNDAY
SPECIAL SOCCER ENDURANCE	SPEED	TACTICS	SOCCER POWER	TACTICS	FRIENDLY MATCH	REST
TACTICS	TACTICS		TACTICS			

In the sixth week, we finish the use of double sessions. Special soccer endurance, speed, and soccer power based on formation, are what we now focus on tactically. Indeed, tactics become our priority. We coach and train our two formations through specialized tactics sessions. With set pieces, we focus on defence: players positioning, behavior, and roles. Our final friendly game is also played; it is a test for the League games, so we play to make it count!

Warm up

6 minutes of running and stretching exercises in the penalty area.

14 minutes of drills designed to improve technique (passing-receiving-heading-body position etc.)

Two teams are in action. The left-hand team stays in position. With the other team, every player moves to the next station after their action. The last player comes around to the start. 3 minutes x 4 repetitions (change roles every 3 minutes).

Main part

Special Soccer Endurance using small sided games. 3vs3vs3 x 3 minutes x 2 sets.

Coaching

The third team, as per the figure above, offers passing options. The team that has possession tries to score on goal. Players should change roles. For a goal to count, the ball needs to be received by an external player before being returned to the centre.

Follow Up Session

A small sided game with two zones (each half is 10 x 30 m.) This is a game for crosses, so only a defender can get into the zone to mark the opposition. In the figure, note how one blue tries to stop two reds. Time 2 x 10 minutes.

Coaching

Emphasis on:

1. Playing the game from the side, and looking to create overloads
2. Additional player movements
3. Creating one-two passing situations and overlaps
4. Attacking and defensive positioning at side kick-offs

Recovery

6 minutes of slow running followed by 6 minutes of stretching.

Warm up

14 minutes of ball coordination work. Two x 6 minutes with a 2 minute break.

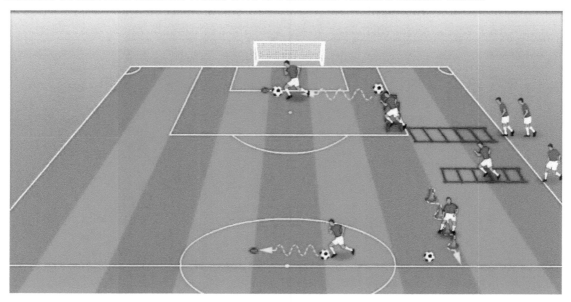

Coordination drills utilising ladders, slaloms, and dribbling.

6 minutes of energetic stretching and running drills.

Main part

Speed work comprised of 4 exercises x 6 repetitions.

1. Skipping 4 m in various formats, then running at speed for 10 m
2. Skipping 4 m alternately back and forth, then sprinting 10 m with change of direction

3. A 5m pass, then a sprint and shot on goal
4. Start with back to goal, before a pass, a sprint, and a shot on goal

Follow Up Session

Tactical game on 2/3 field. Time 12 minutes.

Coaching

Focus on

1. Constant movement to avoid the opposition and find free space; players should offer themselves to the ball holder
2. The diagonal relationship of players
3. Pressure on the ball and the compactness of the defending team
4. Width of the attacking team
5. Transitions should generate immediate reactions and repositioning

Recovery

6 minutes of slow running followed by 6 minutes of passive stretching.

10 minutes of team analysis on a tactics board.

Warm up

25 minutes of group warmups (like a league game).

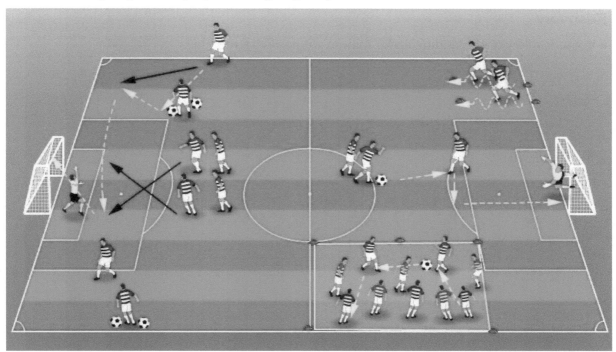

Main part

A tactical game of 11vs11 across the whole field. Time 2 x 30 minutes.

Formations 1-4-3-3 vs 1-4-4-2.

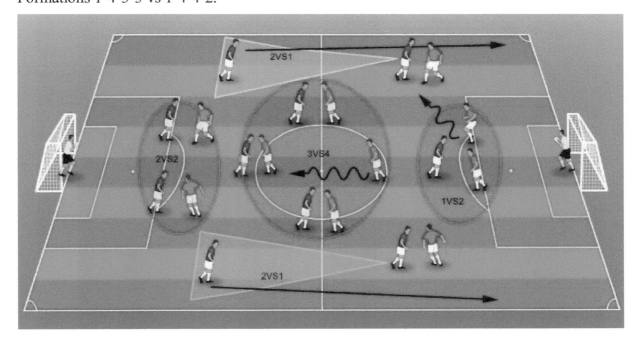

Coaching

Work through each system's weak and strong points.

1-4-3-3: Offensive work of full backs. Cooperation with wide attackers for overloads. The collaboration that three attackers can create. Defensive compactness.

1-4-4-2: Free defender dribbles the ball forward. Holding overload in the centre of the field. Feeding the No "9" for 2vs2 + 1. Opposite movements of two attackers. In defence, check the opposition's full back.

5 minutes of feedback.

Recovery

6 minutes of leisurely running and 6 minutes of passive stretching.

Warm up

6 minutes of energetic stretching drills.

A 14 minute Big box | Little box drill.

The Big Box | Little Box drill is all about improving technique. The inside players run from the small box before any pass or header. Time 4 x 3 minutes. The drill is predominantly about communication; players should instruct teammates where they want the ball: foot, head, etc.

Main part

Soccer power (speed-power) development, based on formation. Total time 40 minutes.

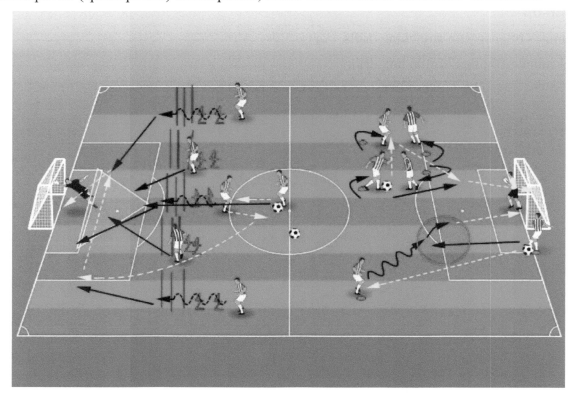

- Drill 1: cooperation of four players and a finishing phase (with 2 defenders or without). 12 minutes
- Drill 2: Offensive and defensive cooperation in 2vs2. 10 minutes

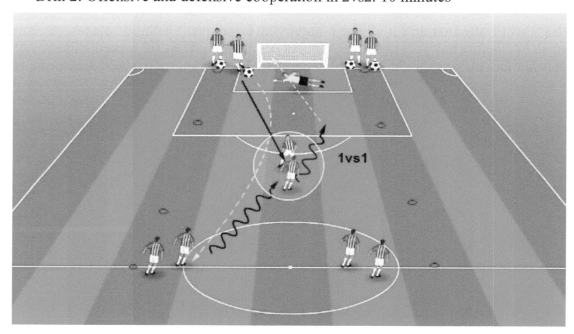

- Drill 3: Long pass-situation 1vs1. 8 minutes

Follow Up Session

Zonal game on a 70 x 60 m field. Time 2 x 10 minutes.

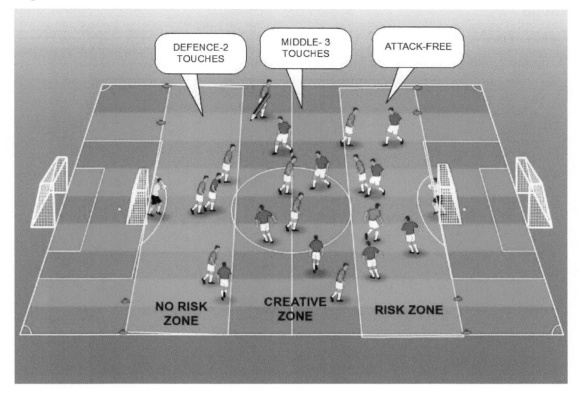

Coaching

Defence: 100% risk avoidance.

Middle zone: Confidence-creating.

Attacking third: Collaboration and risk-taking.

We focus on players making continuous movement, in space, to avoid the opposition. The ball holder is offered diagonal relationships to other players, whilst being pressured on the ball by the defence. The defending team should be compact, and the attacking team should look to utilize width. An emphasis should be placed on transitions creating immediate reactions and repositioning from players.

Recovery

6 minutes of slow running then 6 minutes of passive stretching.

Warm up

6 minutes of active stretching.

A 14 minute passing game using a 1-4-4-2 formation.

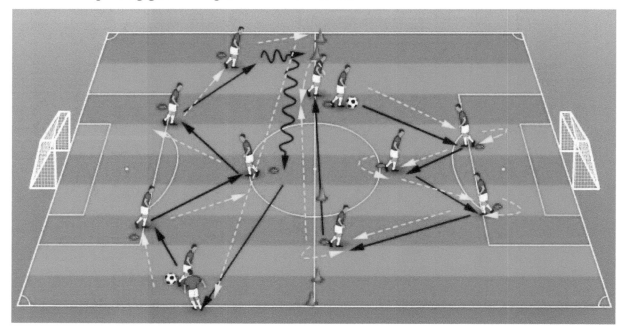

Pass and follow. The last player dribbles to the start. Focus on passing quality, and body position for receiving the ball. Change the player order after 6 minutes.

Main part

Working on reaction speed. 6 m x 6 x 2 sets.

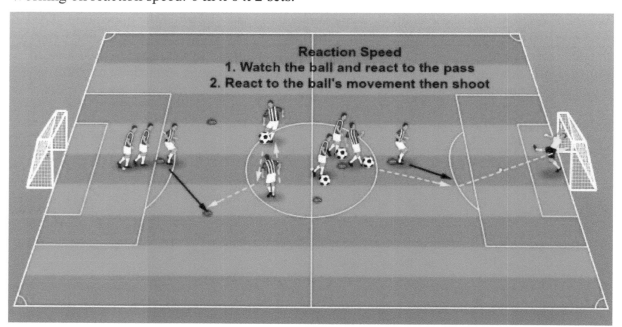

Exercise 1: Two players pass to each other 2-3 times then pass to a cone. The player reacts to get the ball before the cone.

Exercise 2: The player has the ball at his back and reacts to the pass in order to shoot.

Follow Up Session

Set piece training.

This follow up focuses on corner kicks in an 11vs11 approach. After the corner kick is taken, play continues until the ball goes dead (goal, save, throw in, counter attack) or until the coach stops the game. Time 20 minutes.

Recovery

6 minutes of slow running followed by 6 minutes of passive stretching.

Session 46 | Saturday | Friendly Game

Championship approach in terms of player selection. Limited Substitutions, in relation to the needs of the game.

We treat the game, like a normal League game!

Defensive function:

1. Defenders push up the pitch - 10 m before the centre line!
2. The ball holder is always pressured. Teammates provide diagonal cover and communicate with each other!
3. Make sure there is balance in any defensive overload (keep at least three defenders behind the ball, and always have more defenders than attackers)
4. Immediate reactions when the ball goes loose. Defensive transition
5. Emphasis on 1vs1. "Fighters-winners"!

Attacking play:

1. Players mobility and movement, on and off the ball
2. Using width to create space
3. Support for teammates in possession
4. Shots on goal are a priority

Formation 1-4-2-3-1

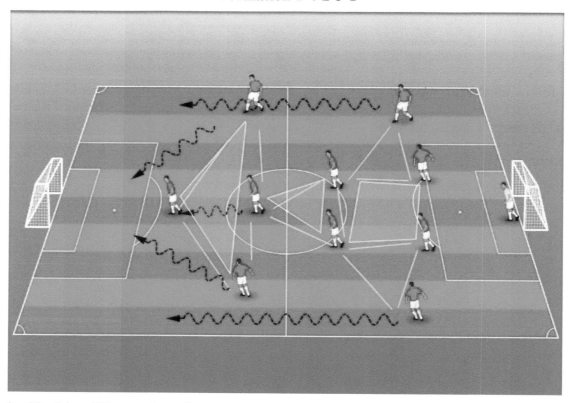

1. No 9 is a "Target player"
2. In 1-4-2-3-1, the three players ahead of the "No 9" need to change their positions
3. These three players also need to move to find space behind the defence (between defenders)
4. Full backs exploit space in attack
5. Employ the various set pieces that have been trained previously

Final positions-zones in attack (below)

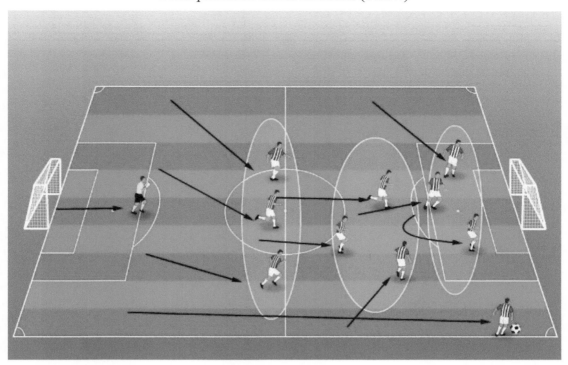

Defensive formation 1-4-4-1-1

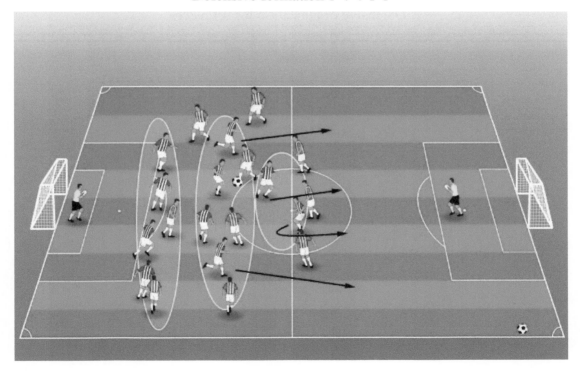

Positions of players in defence, for corner-kicks (below)

Defensive organization for set pieces

Day 42 | Sunday | Rest

Week 7

MONDAY	TUESDAY	WEDNESDAY	THURSDAY	FRIDAY	SATURDAY	SUNDAY
BASIC SOCCER ENDURANCE	REST	SOCCER-SPEED	TACTICS	REACTION SPEED	REST	League Game
TACTICS		SPECIAL SOCCER ENDURANCE		TACTICS		
		TACTICS				

The seventh week has the look of the season, and brings the players and the team as close as possible to "Championship" operations. The coaching emphasis is on team tactics, the two main formations, and set pieces. Tactics are developed and evolved in anticipation of the first official Championship game.

Warm up

A 2 x 8 minute passing game with fixed formations and passive defences over 2/3 of the field. Have a 4 minute break in the middle of the game, with active stretching.

The two teams play a possession game with pre-planned tactical moves during attacking build ups and passive "space defence" defending. Change players' roles after 8 minutes. Use three zones to help players fully develop their movement(s) and the role(s). The defending team should stay close and compact; the attacking team should have depth and width.

Build up moves:

1. The four defenders should try to force the attackers to change their side of attack (e.g., force the attacking team onto their weaker side)
2. In attack, the full back should look to cooperate with the wide attacker
3. Wide attackers should cooperate with the No 9 and No 10
4. The No 10 should move in behind the No 9 back (to act as a hidden attacker)

Main part

8 minutes of mobility and flexibility. Then a 30 minute aggressive shadow game with finishing phases over the whole field. Use two teams of 11 x 11. Five variations can be used.

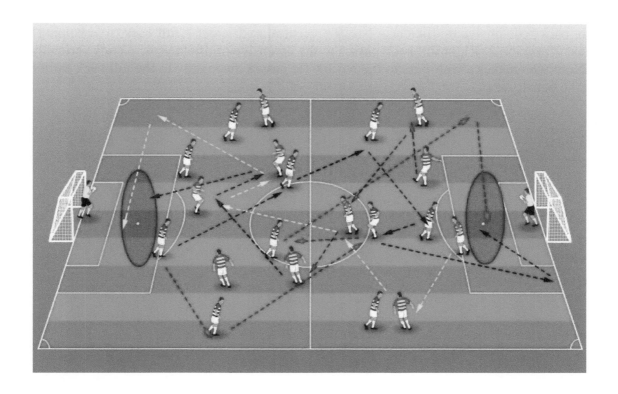

(Passing order) Left back > left central defender > defensive midfielder – diagonal to right full back (overlapping) passes. Variation 1: The left back passes to a central defender; he passes to the defensive midfielder who passes to the other full back (right) who makes a cross into the penalty area.

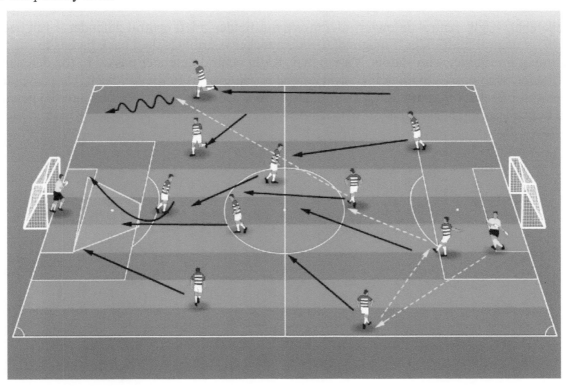

Right back > defensive midfielder > No "9" > central midfielder > full back (overlapping) – passes. Variation 2: Right full back passes to the defensive midfielder; he passes vertically to the No 9 who makes a wall-pass to the No 10. He passes diagonally to the full back for a cross into the penalty area.

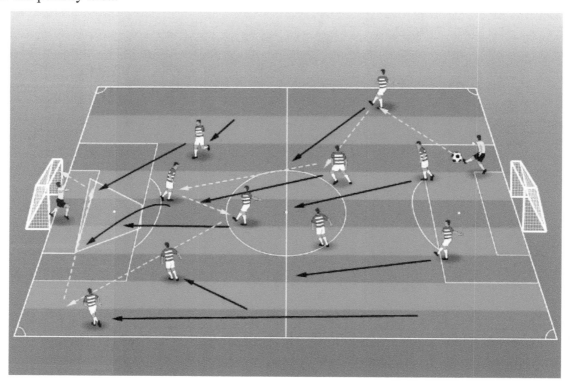

Goalkeeper >right central defender> defensive midfielder > left central defender > full back > No "9" > central midfielder > diagonal to side attacker > dribbles then back passes to upcoming midfielder who shoots. Variation 3: Right central defender passes to the defensive midfielder, who passes to the left central defender who passes to the full back. He passes to No 9 who offers a wall pass to No 10. He passes to a wide attacker who runs into the penalty area before passing back to No 10 who shoots.

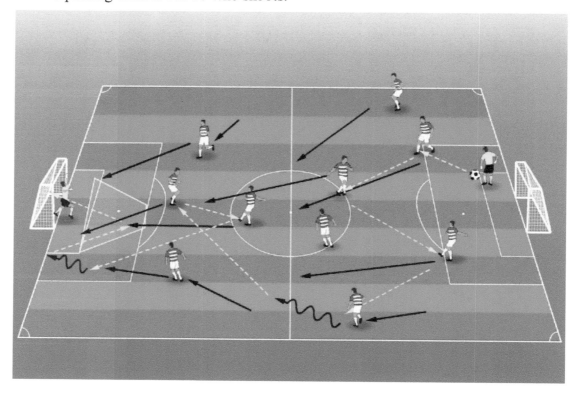

Goalkeeper > full back > defensive midfielder. Variation 4: The central defender passes to the defensive midfielder, who plays a long ball to the defending team's weak side for the wide attacker. The attacker crosses into the penalty area.

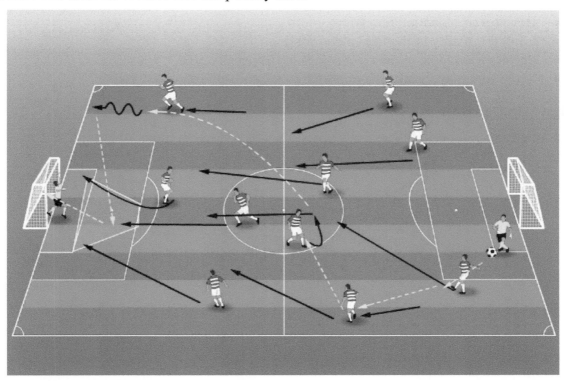

Full back > defensive midfielder > No 9 > central midfielder > hidden player behind the No 9. Variation 5: The full back passes to the defensive midfielder, who passes to No 9 who provides a wall pass to No 10. A vertical pass follows for an attacker who runs behind No 9 (hidden attacker) who then shoots on goal.

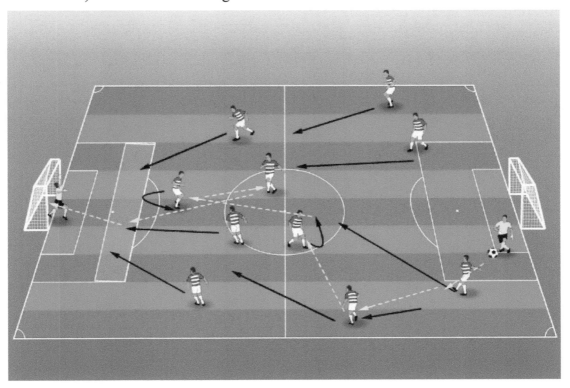

Coaching

- Focus on the quality of passing
- Focus on body position for receiving the ball in direction of play
- Develop combination play
- Look for quality in the final pass/crossing
- Players need to be in the right places in the penalty area
- Make sure players take the opportunity to score, and shoot on goal

Follow Up Session

An 8 minute running drill (30 seconds fast, 30 seconds slow) in three subgroups.

Recovery

4 minutes of slow running followed by 6 minutes of passive stretching

Session 48 | Wednesday

Warm up

6 minutes of energetic stretching in one quarter of the pitch, responding to the coach's orders, while moving a ball in pairs.

14 minutes of coordinated drills with a ball.

Slaloms, jumping, passing, ladder and side moves. Time 2 x 6 minutes. Change drills in the middle.

Main part

Developing soccer speed power for 30 minutes.

Developing soccer power through shooting drills.

1. Pass, slalom and jumps, then shoot x 4
2. Heading and slalom, then shoot x 4
3. Pass, side jumps, and sprint, then shoot x 4

Follow Up Session

Formation-based soccer focusing on speed; in 5vs4 and 4vs3 situations (2 x 6 minute sessions). Time to attack: 20 seconds.

Follow Up Session II

Tactical game 11vs11 across the whole field. Formations 1-4-2-3-1 and 1-4-3-3. Time 15 minutes.

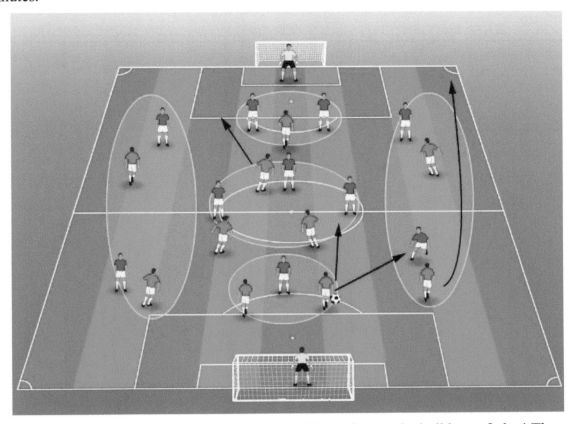

The second central midfielder (in both formations) is the key to the build-up of play! The central defenders look to dribble up the pitch, then they try to engage an opposition midfielder before passing to a teammate (maybe a full back or a central midfielder)

Recovery

6 minutes of slow running and 6 minutes of stretching.

Session 49 | Thursday

10 minutes of tactical analysis/explanation on a tactics board.

Warm up

A 25 minute exercise-based warm up that incorporates crossing, shooting, running, and rondo.

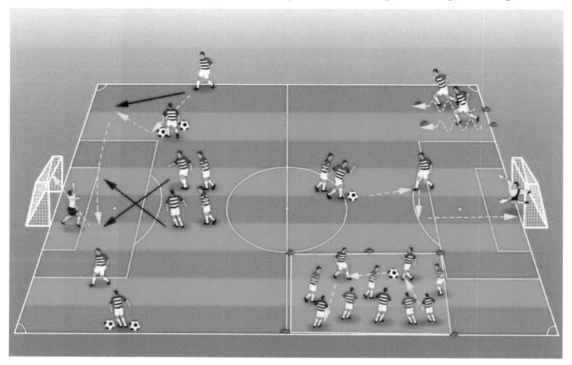

Main part

Tactical game with 11vs11 across the whole field. Two 25 minute halves.

Formations 1-4-3-3 vs 1-4-4-2

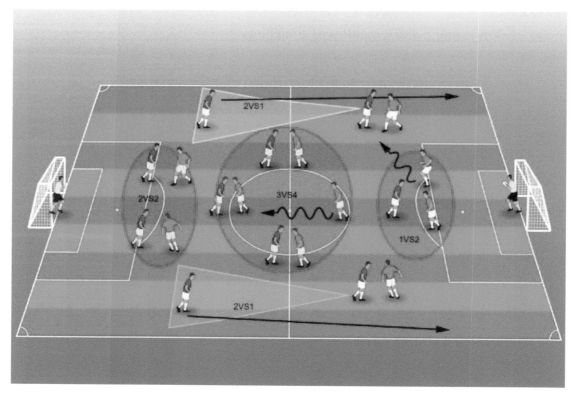

Coaching

- Focus on identifying the strong and weak points for each system with the players you have.
- 1-4-3-3: Try to play the full back in the attacking half to make a 2vs1 overload (full back and wide attacker). The collaborative efforts of the 3 attackers. Shutting up shop at the back.
- 1-4-4-2: Exploitation of free central defender. Developing and maintaining overloads in the center. Getting the ball to the No "9" for 2vs2 + 1. No 9 Movement in and out, front and back. In defence, we look out for the opposition's full backs. Our No 10 returns to the middle of the pitch, whilst a midfielder moves close to the side lines to mark the full back.
- 5 minutes of feedback.

Recovery

6 minutes of slow running followed by 6 minutes of passive stretching.

Warm up

6 minutes of energetic stretching, alongside a 14 minute Rondo, 5vs2.

Main part

Reaction speed training for 10 minutes.

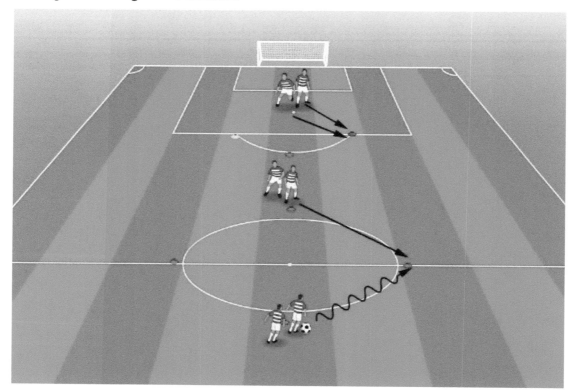

1. In pairs, players must sprint to cones of the colour called by the coach (six repetitions).
2. In pairs, the player with the ball makes a sudden dribbling move to the left or right. The other play must react to the move!

Follow Up Session

Set pieces for 20 minutes.

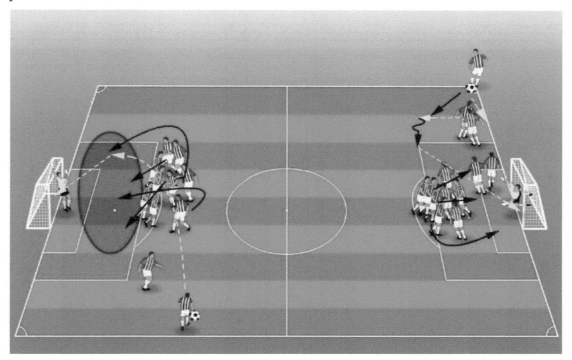

Attacking corners with variations:

1. The ball is returned to the player who took the corner, who then shoots on goal.
2. A pass is made to a player who is – initially – out of range but who subsequently shoots.

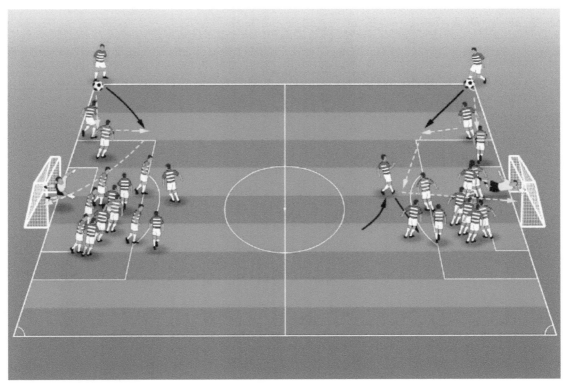

3. The player taking the corner kick passes to his teammate, comes inside the field, and receives the ball back. At this point, he either shoots for a goal, or passes to a teammate who has moved out of the penalty area for their own shot on goal.

4. A screen is created to help a teammate avoid marking. In doing this, an attacker moves to second post for a heading or shot on goal option.

Follow Up Session II

10 minutes of crossing and finishing in pairs. Make it competitive; which partnership can score the most goals?

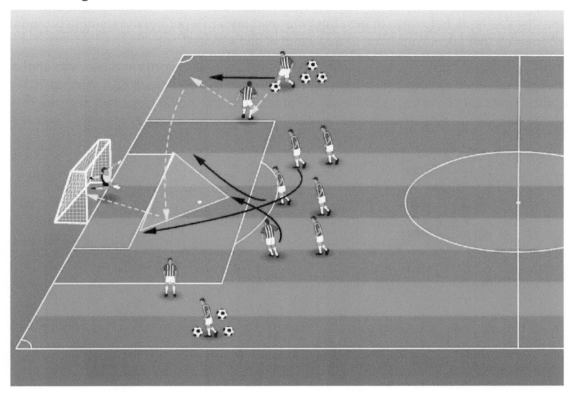

Recovery

6 minutes of slow running followed by 6 minutes of passive stretching.

Saturday | First Championship Game!

Sunday | Rest

Epilogue

So, there you have it. The pre-season training routine that led us to the championship.

I hope that this book helps you to develop your own effective pre-season training programme. A programme that takes your team to new heights and success!

It would be a grave omission, on my part, if I did not say a few words to those who applied all the things that this book describes. My players, the team of Paleochora F.C. who, in 2016-17, gave their souls for the team; together we accomplished something great and historic!

Thank you!

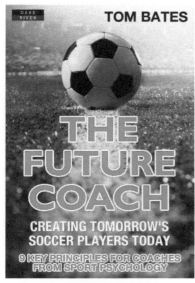

DARK RIVER

TOM BATES

THE FUTURE COACH

CREATING TOMORROW'S SOCCER PLAYERS TODAY

9 KEY PRINCIPLES FOR COACHES FROM SPORT PSYCHOLOGY

PLAY LIKE PEP GUARDIOLA'S BARCELONA

A Soccer Coach's Guide

Agustín Peraita

The English translation of the Spanish bestseller "Quiere que mi equipo juegue como el F.C.Barcelona de Guardiola"

Foreword by Ray Power

DEVELOPING SOCCER PLAYERS
FORWARD-SPECIFIC PRACTICES

DAN BOLAS

DARK RIVER

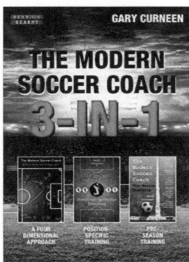

BENNION KEARNY

GARY CURNEEN

THE MODERN SOCCER COACH 3-IN-1

A FOUR DIMENSIONAL APPROACH — **POSITION-SPECIFIC TRAINING** — **PRE-SEASON TRAINING**

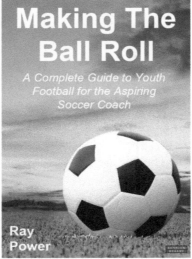

Making The Ball Roll

A Complete Guide to Youth Football for the Aspiring Soccer Coach

Ray Power

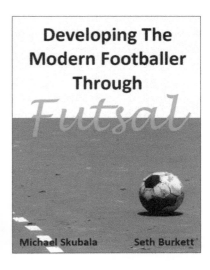

Developing The Modern Footballer Through *Futsal*

Michael Skubala   **Seth Burkett**

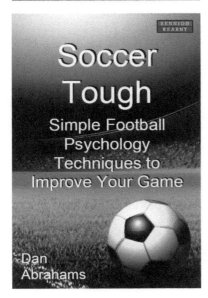

BENNION KEARNY

Soccer Tough

Simple Football Psychology Techniques to Improve Your Game

Dan Abrahams

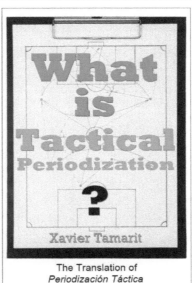

What is Tactical Periodization

?

Xavier Tamarit

The Translation of *Periodización Táctica*

Confidence · Commitment · Communication · Concentration · Control

5Cs

Coaching Psychological Skills in Youth Football

Developing The 5Cs

Chris Harwood
Richard Anderson

Deliberate Soccer Practice

50 Defending Football Exercises to Improve Decision-Making

Ray Power

101 GOALKEEPER TRAINING PRACTICES

> Warm-Ups
> Individual GK Practices
> Small GK Group Practices
> Team-Based Practices

ANDY ELLERAY

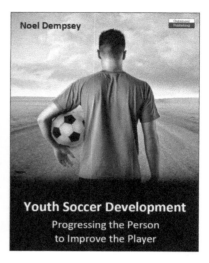

Noel Dempsey

Youth Soccer Development

Progressing the Person to Improve the Player

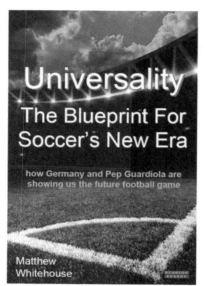

Universality

The Blueprint For Soccer's New Era

how Germany and Pep Guardiola are showing us the future football game

Matthew Whitehouse

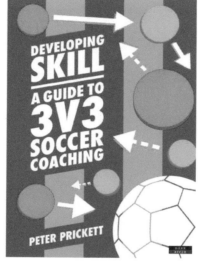

DEVELOPING SKILL

A GUIDE TO 3V3 SOCCER COACHING

PETER PRICKETT

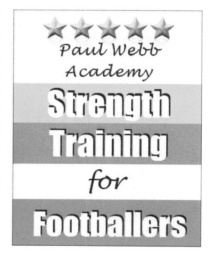

★★★★★
Paul Webb Academy

Strength Training *for* Footballers

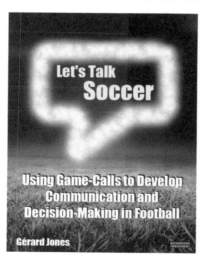

Let's Talk Soccer

Using Game-Calls to Develop Communication and Decision-Making in Football

Gérard Jones

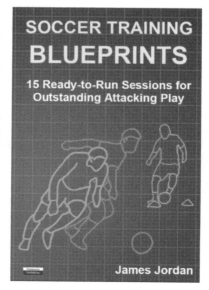

SOCCER TRAINING BLUEPRINTS

15 Ready-to-Run Sessions for Outstanding Attacking Play

James Jordan

WINNING YOUR PLAYERS

THROUGH TRUST, LOYALTY, AND RESPECT

DeAngelo Wiser

www.BennionKearny.com/soccer